TRAVEL THE WORLD IN CROSS STITCH

LESLEY TEARE

D&C
David and Charles

www.mycraftivity.com

For my friend Tina

A DAVID & CHARLES BOOK
Copyright © David & Charles Limited 2008

David & Charles is an F+W Publications Inc. company
4700 East Galbraith Road
Cincinnati, OH 45236

First published in the UK in 2006
First paperback edition 2008

Text and designs copyright © Lesley Teare 2006

Lesley Teare has asserted her right to be identified as author of this work in accordance
with the Copyright, Designs and Patents Act, 1988.

A catalogue record for this book is available from the British Library.

ISBN-13: 978-0-7153-2242-0 hardback
ISBN-10: 0-7153-2242-7 hardback
ISBN-13: 978-0-7153-2993-1 paperback
ISBN-10: 0-7153-2993-6 paperback

Printed in China by SNP Leefung
for David & Charles
Brunel House   Newton Abbot   Devon

Executive Editor: Cheryl Brown
Desk Editor: Ame Verso
Project Editor: Juliet Bracken
Art Editor: Prudence Rogers
Production Controller: Roslyn Napper
Photography: Kim Sayer and Karl Adamson

Visit our website at www.davidandcharles.co.uk

David & Charles books are available from all good bookshops; alternatively you can contact our
Orderline on 0870 9908222 or write to us at FREEPOST EX2 110, D&C Direct, Newton Abbot, TQ12 4ZZ
(no stamp required UK only); US customers call 800-289-0963 and Canadian customers call 800-840-5220.

ACKNOWLEDGMENTS

Although we have worked closely together on many designs, this is the first large project that Tina Godwin and I have tackled together on our own. My heartfelt appreciation, Tina, for the hours of stitching and for working to such tight deadlines. Your expertise and unerring attention to detail and, in particular, your enthusiasm has made this project a very enjoyable one.

A special thanks goes to Cheryl Brown at David & Charles for steering me in the right direction on such a challenging book, offering advice but also allowing me the time to find the answers I was looking for. And to everyone else who has worked so hard at David & Charles including Ame Verso, Prudence Rogers, Lin Clements, who has again produced such wonderful charts, and Juliet Bracken for editing my text.

My thanks to Michael Oxley at the Art and Framing Centre in Witham for his expert advice and framing skills. And not forgetting Myke, my husband, whose knowledge has been invaluable in talking through the geographical queries that arose.

However I have to acknowledge that the real tribute for this book goes to this remarkable, spectacular and beautiful planet of ours that we hold in trust to care for, so that future generations will also be able to wonder at this world around us.

CONTENTS

INTRODUCTION

L et me take you on a journey around the different countries and cultures of the world. *Travel the World in Cross Stitch* contains over 500 colourful and varied designs from six continents. Whether you want to remember a country you have visited, wish a friend bon voyage, or make a gift for someone special, dip into this fascinating collection to stitch the world around us.

Each chapter captures in stitches some of the people, landscapes, wildlife, sites, symbols and customs of that continent. The Sydney Opera House, Native American art, the Taj Mahal and the big cats of Africa are just a few of the designs I hope will inspire you.

You can either stitch a large design that brings together several of these images or choose from the library of small motifs that follows it. I have shown you a selection of fun, quick

cards and gifts you can make with the designs, including a postcard mounted on a card backing to send to friends back home.

I have tried to pick key sights from around the world and can only apologize if I have missed out your favourite. Although I have made every effort to be faithful to the original images, at times I have used artistic licence to create the best possible design. On designs which have blocks of stitches in a single colour you can save time by choosing a fabric to match the thread colour and leave these areas blank.

It has been a challenge to pick so few images to portray the feel and culture of each vast continent, but I hope it goes some way towards depicting in cross stitch this wonderful world we live in.

Start Stitching Now

Here is the basic stitching information you need to get started on making the designs in this book. For more detailed finishing instructions turn to pages 103–104. The designs are worked on either 14-count Aida or 28-count evenweave fabrics, unless otherwise stated. The following stitching principles apply:

✓ Prepare your fabric for stitching by hemming or binding the edges and by folding it in half each way to find the centre. Mark this point with a stitch.

✓ Begin in the centre on both the chart and your fabric, and work outwards across the design, making a cross stitch for each square on the chart.

✓ When stitching on 14-count Aida, work each cross stitch over one block of the fabric following the diagram above right. On 28-count evenweave, work each cross

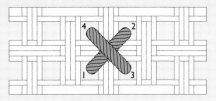

Single cross stitch on Aida

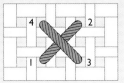

Single cross stitch on evenweave

stitch over two fabric threads as shown above. Use a size 24 tapestry needle on 14-count and a size 26 on 28-count.

✓ Use two strands of cotton for the cross stitch and one strand for the backstitch, unless otherwise stated. Refer to the chart key for which shades of stranded cotton and metallic thread to use.

✓ Some of the charts also include three-quarter cross stitches (also known as fractional stitches). They appear on the chart as triangles and are worked as shown below. On Aida you will need to piece a hole in the centre of the block to go down through.

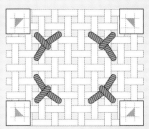

Three-quarter cross stitch on evenweave

✓ When all the stitching is complete, carefully wash the fabric if necessary before pressing it face down into a towel.

✓ Prepare your design for framing or finish off your gift following the instructions on pages 103–104.

EUROPE

Europe is a continent of many nations, each with its own distinct culture and history, and for centuries a favourite destination for travellers. I made the European Tour the theme for the main design in this chapter. This is built up from a patchwork of images representing the different countries of Europe that might have been visited on a Grand Tour. For example, there is the Eiffel Tower in Paris, beautiful Venice with its Gondoliers and a St Bernard dog with a brandy flask around its neck, ready to save lives in the Alps. The motifs are placed, with a little artistic licence, in roughly the right place on the map of Europe. This makes it easy to pick one out to stitch as a quick card or gift.

There are plenty of other small charts to choose from, with suggestions on ways to use them. You can make a cheerful farewell card for a friend featuring bright sunflowers, a traditional Welsh bookmark for St David's Day, or a stylish mobile phone pouch decorated with a lemon branch motif. I added a misty view of Venice to an album for holiday snapshots and made a pincushion with an Eastern European motif a fellow stitcher will love. A Russian doll was the ideal decoration for a pencil holder.

For those who still prefer the challenge of a bigger project, I have included a gastronomic sampler to celebrate the French nation's love of food that will make a charming framed picture for a kitchen. These motifs can be swapped with some of the images from the other pages. So let's get ready to begin our European tour...

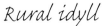

Rural idyll

This postcard design of the English countryside makes a delightful quick card. Stitch it on white Aida, trim the fabric six holes away from the edge of the design and pull out a few threads all round to make a fringe. Stick it to a 5 x 8cm (2 x 3in) piece of green card with double-sided tape.
Design size 4.5 x 7cm (1¾ x 2¾in) **Stitch count** 26 x 39

European Tour

The main design for this chapter features a selection of images from across Europe and is stitched on white Aida. Work the cross stitch before adding the backstitch outlines and count the squares carefully when moving to start a new motif. Press your completed stitching carefully and frame as a picture.
Design size 18.2 x 24.5cm (7½ x 9⅜in) **Stitch count** 103 x 134

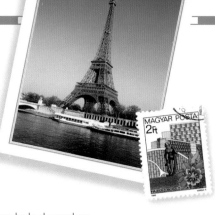

Exploring Europe

Welsh pride

Make a fun bookmark with three famous Welsh symbols charted on page 13. The design was stitched on white Aida, trimmed four squares away from the edge of the design on three sides, and 10 squares below the design. Fringe the edges by pulling out a few threads on three sides and enough horizontal threads below the design to leave two blank Aida squares all round.

Design size 10 x 4.5cm (4 x 1¾in) **Stitch count** 55 x 24

Entente cordiale

Make a cheerful card using the bright sunflower motif on page 15. Stitch the design on white Aida and mount it in a yellow card with a 10 x 6.5cm (4 x 2½in) aperture.

Design size 9.5 x 6cm (3¾ x 2¼in) **Stitch count** 54 x 30

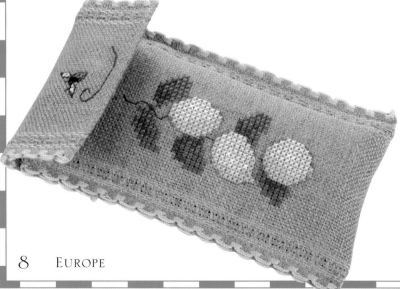

Good to talk

Make a handy pouch to hold a mobile phone using the lemon motif from the chart on page 14. The design was stitched on a natural linen band and made into a pouch as explained on page 104. Stitch the small bee from the same chart on the flap to disguise the position of the popper.

Design size 7.5 x 3.3cm (3 x 1¼in) **Stitch count** 40 x 18

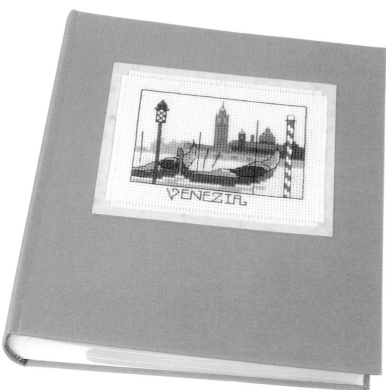

Romantic Venice

Decorate your holiday album with the romantic view of Venice charted on page 16. The design was stitched on cream Aida and mounted on a 8 x 11.5cm (3 x 4½in) piece of cream card. Fringe your trimmed design by pulling out a few threads all round, and use double-sided tape to stick the layers together.

Design size 7.5 x 10cm (3 x 4in)
Stitch count 40 x 56

Stitcher's gift

Make a pretty pincushion or sachet using the quick and easy Eastern European motif from page 24. The design was stitched on red evenweave fabric and made into a pincushion as explained on page 104.

Design size 3cm (1¼in) square **Stitch count** 16 x 16

Russian doll

Make a special gift for a child by stitching their name and one of the Russian doll motifs on page 25 as a decoration for a pencil holder. The design was stitched on white Aida band and the two ends joined in a seam to fit the pencil holder. See page 102 for a backstitch alphabet to personalize the gift.

Design size Doll only 4.5 x 2cm (1¾ x ¾in) **Stitch count** 25 x 11

European Tour
DMC stranded cotton
Cross stitch

- ● blanc
- 157
- 164
- ● 167
- 168
- 209
- 301
- ◉ 310
- 535
- 613
- 704
- 743
- ○ 744
- 746
- 799
- 772
- 905
- 945
- 3801
- \ 3823
- 3828
- 3853

Backstitch
— 310
— 898
— 3801

French knots
● 898

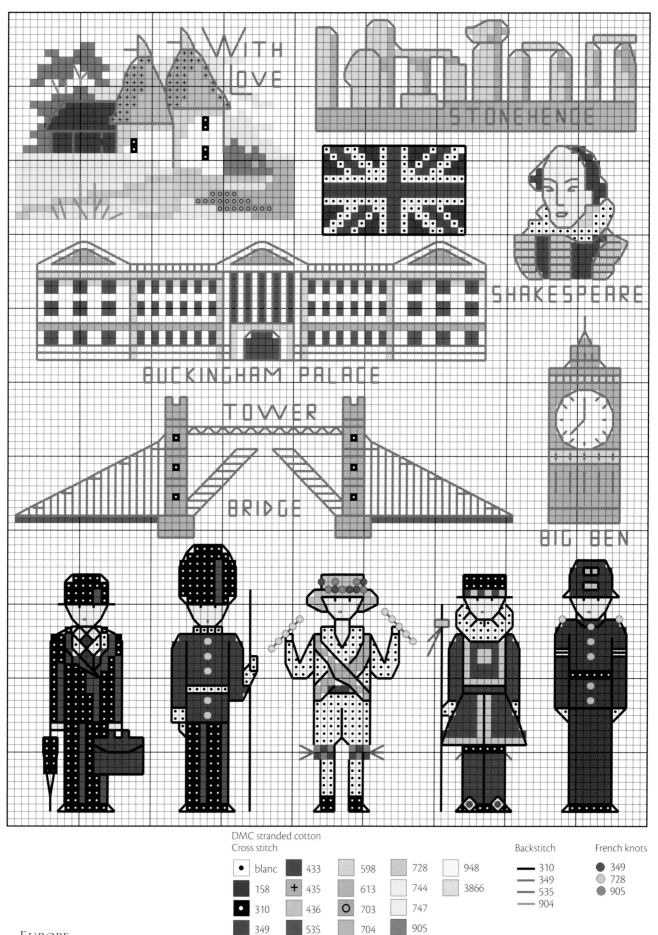

WITH LOVE

STONEHENGE

SHAKESPEARE

BUCKINGHAM PALACE

TOWER

BRIDGE

BIG BEN

DMC stranded cotton
Cross stitch

• blanc	433	598	728	948
158	+ 435	613	744	3866
⊙ 310	436	⊙ 703	747	
349	535	704	905	

Backstitch
— 310
— 349
— 535
— 904

French knots
● 349
● 728
● 905

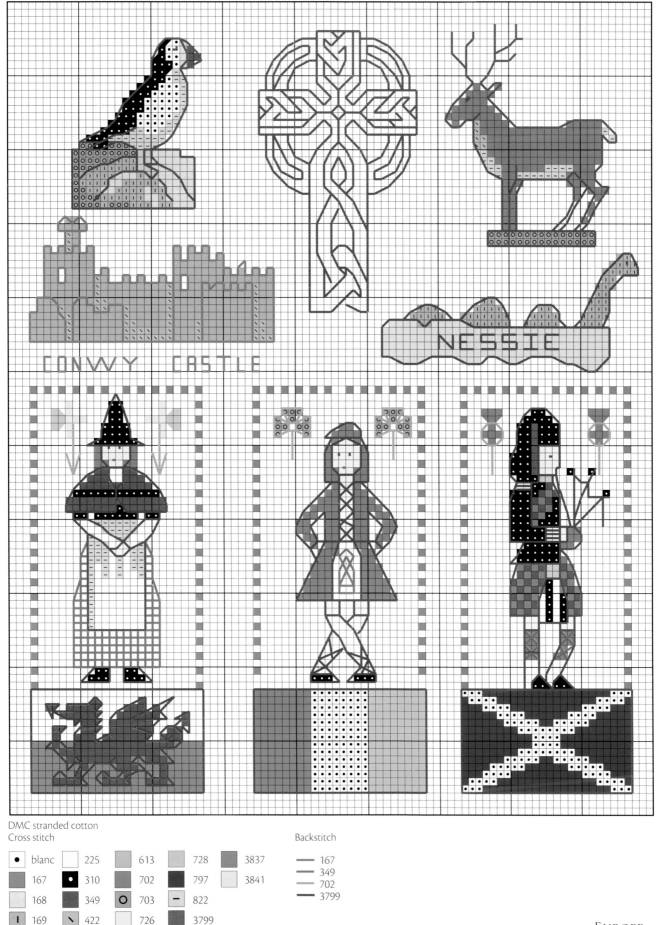

CONWY CASTLE

NESSIE

DMC stranded cotton
Cross stitch

● blanc	☐ 225	613	728	3837
167	▦ 310	702	797	3841
168	349	⊙ 703	− 822	
I 169	╲ 422	726	3799	

Backstitch

— 167
— 349
— 702
— 3799

DMC stranded cotton
Cross stitch

Backstitch

● blanc	⊙ 349	420	＼ 676	❙ 814	⊙ 3346	3776
⊙ 164	351	422	＋ 677	945		3347
／ 307	368	445	680	❙ 3047		3685
⊡ 310	402	524	746	3345		3687

Backstitch
— 433
— 3347

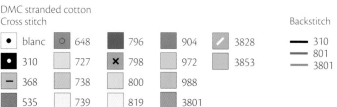

DMC stranded cotton
Cross stitch

Backstitch

•	blanc	○	648		796		904	╱	3828
▪	310		727	✕	798		972		3853
─	368		738		800		988	
	535		739		819		3801	

— 310
— 801
— 3801

ITALIA

PISA

PUGLIA

ROMA

FIRENZE

SIENNA

VENEZIA

VATICAN CITY

DMC stranded cotton
Cross stitch

• blanc	612	I 746	L 922	╱ 3012	3756
− 301	✕ 613	826	◀ 926	3013	3768
350	677	◀ 830	927	⦿ 3021	◆ 3866
402	700	912	3011	╲ 3033	

Backstitch

blanc

——— 3021

——— 3768

CARNWAL

OLD TOWN
SAN MORINO

DAVID

DMC stranded cotton
Cross stitch

	162		413		553		813		895	→	3828
T	164		422		677	/	814	Δ	3046	V	3853
⊡	310		743		702	●	827	O	3712	·	3865
	350	I	746	+	703		869		3826	/	5282 metallic

Backstitch

— 310

— 869

SEGRADA

BUENOS
DIAS

BOM
DIA

FAMILIA

ALHAMBRA

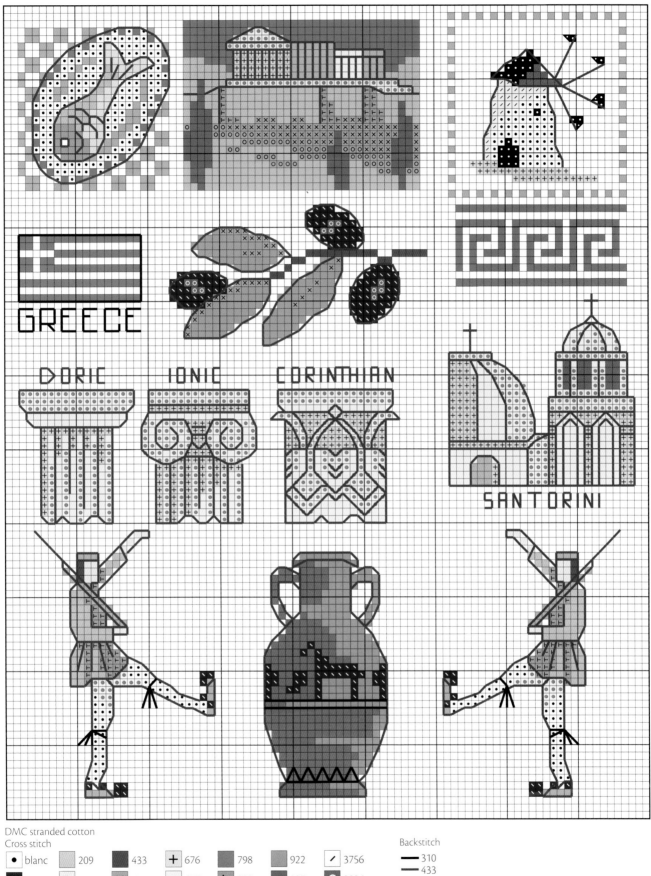

GREECE

DORIC   IONIC   CORINTHIAN

SANTORINI

DMC stranded cotton
Cross stitch

● blanc		433
154	211	× 471
162	● 310	472
163	350	535

+ 676	798	922
677	⊢ 832	937
● 712	834	951
729	921	O 989

/ 3756	
◎ 3834	

Backstitch
— 310
— 433

DMC stranded cotton
Cross stitch

• blanc	▪ 310	720
164	340	818
167	T 402	O 989
301	517	▽ 3045

L 3046	L 3776	3842
3047	V 3820	3852
3747	⊥ 3821	
/ 3756	3823	

Backstitch
— 938

French knots
● 3852

DMC stranded cotton
Cross stitch

● blanc	164	433	I 728	∧ 945	3747	
ecru	310	I 434	648	951	3746	
155		436	▬ 918	O 989		
/ 156	350	535	937	‒ 3024		

Backstitch
— 310
— 350
— 535
— 801

BRUGES

LUXEMBOURG   BELGIUM   NETHERLANDS

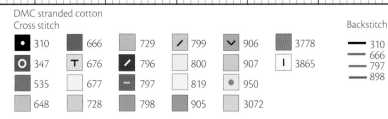

DMC stranded cotton
Cross stitch

						Backstitch
▪ 310	▪ 666	729	╱ 799	∨ 906	3778	── 310
⊙ 347	T 676	╱ 796	800	907	I 3865	── 666
535	677	─ 797	819	• 950		── 797
648	728	798	905	3072		── 898

NORWAY•SWEDEN•DENMARK•FINLAND•ICELAND

NORWEGIAN FJORD

DMC stranded cotton
Cross stitch

• blanc	519	613	793	904	3747
155	666	722	797	948	
156	610	725	798	○ 3347	
310	612	738	918	3348	

Backstitch
— blanc
— 310
— 433
— 666

French knots
● 666

DMC stranded cotton
Cross stitch

		Backstitch
• blanc	⌐ 422	⌐ 739	772	V 3828	blanc
225	⌐ 703	743	869	3839	349
• 310	712	∧ 744	905	5282 metallic	938
— 349	← 738	λ 746	+ 3779		

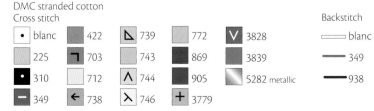

FROM RUSSIA WITH LOVE

DMC stranded cotton
Cross stitch

· 310	→ 648	803	O 844	L 920	5282 metallic		
− 322	728	\ 817	895	922			
349	× 761	819	△ 905	3753			
434	/ 801	822	906	I 3865			

Backstitch

—— 310

—— 801

—— 905

—— 5282 metallic

French knots

● 310

● 666

◐ 5282 metallic

NORTH AMERICA

North America is a vast continent that extends from the Arctic wilderness to the shores of the Caribbean. Here you will find every kind of natural environment, from forests and mountains to deserts and swamps, as well as bustling cities like New York and Los Angeles. I set out to show some of this diversity in my North American picture, 'Cherish Your Dreams'. I also included several distinctive American icons: a dream circle to symbolize Native American culture, the Statue of Liberty for modern America and finally the Bald Eagle, to symbolize the mighty United States.

Throughout the rest of the chapter you will find a wide range of motifs depicting North American places, traditions and culture, and my suggestions for gifts to make with them. There is another sampler of Native American designs on page 44, and a series of Canadian images on pages 32 and 33.

You will find plenty of patriotic designs that are ideal for bright, quick postcards or greetings cards, and a fun gift to make for a friend who's just visited New York. By contrast, the New England church motif with its mellow, autumnal colours looks perfect mounted on a dainty miniature bell pull. And the monochromatic detail of Washington and the White House on page 35 makes a striking and unusual design, especially if you stitch it on a raw linen fabric.

Fans will love the images of Marilyn Monroe and Elvis, which are perfect for the cover of an autograph album, and the other motifs of country and western music, and jazz from the Deep South. So now it's time to begin our North American journey…

'Have a nice day' postcard

Make this postcard with its familiar greeting as a quick card for friends in America. Stitch the design on white Aida, trim the fabric six holes away from the edge of the design and pull out a few threads all round in a fringe. Stick it to a 8 x 5cm (3 x 2in) piece of red card.
Design size 4.5 x 7.5cm (1¾ x 2⅞in) **Stitch count** 24 x 40

Cherish Your Dreams

The main picture for this chapter incorporates two North American icons, the Statue of Liberty and the Bald Eagle, and is stitched over two threads on Zweigart Jazlyn linen in cream. Work all the cross stitch before adding the backstitch outlines, press your work carefully and frame as a picture.
Design size 19.5 x 23.5cm (7¾ x 9¼in) **Stitch count** 108 x 130

STATESIDE STITCHING

Liberty Bell

This bright design of Liberty Bell, charted on page 34, makes a delightful card on an American theme. The design was stitched on white Aida and mounted in a matching blue card with a 8 x 5cm (3⅛ x 2in) aperture.

Design size 7.5 x 4.5cm (2⅞ x 1¾in) **Stitch count** 40 x 24

New York, New York

Here's a fun, quick gift to remember a visit to the Big Apple by. The motif was stitched on white plastic canvas, trimmed to leave one blank canvas bar all round the design and attached to the cap with velcro.

Design size 3.8 x 4.2cm (1½ x 1¾in) **Stitch count** 21 x 23

Floral signature

Personalize a gift with this pretty floral tag from page 43, or tie the tag to the handle of your suitcase to make it stand out. The design was stitched on white Aida and trimmed to fit a tag cut from purple card. Use double-sided tape to attach it to the tag and punch a hole in the top for threading ribbon through.

Design size 4.5 x 6.2cm (1¾ x 2½in) **Stitch count** 24 x 34

Autograph this

Decorate the cover of an autograph book with this famous Marilyn Monroe pose. The design was stitched on sky blue Aida, trimmed and fringed by pulling out a few threads on each side, before being attached to the book cover with double-sided tape. The Elvis motif on page 42 would look good here, too.

Design size 9.5 x 3.9cm (3¾ x 1½in)

Stitch count 51 x 21

Stunning in black

A black linen evenweave fabric provides the perfect contrast for this pink Hibiscus flower from page 45. The design makes a lovely gift mounted in a 9cm (3½in) black ceramic trinket pot. Stitch the design over two threads when using evenweave fabric.

Design size of the flower 5.5 x 5cm (2¼ x 2in)

Stitch count for the flower 30 x 27

New England colours

This picture of a New England church makes a delightful mini bell pull. The design was stitched on a 10cm (4in) wide white Aida band and sewn on to wooden bell pull ends (see page 104).

Design size 8 x 7.5cm (3¼ x 3in) **Stitch count** 44 x 42

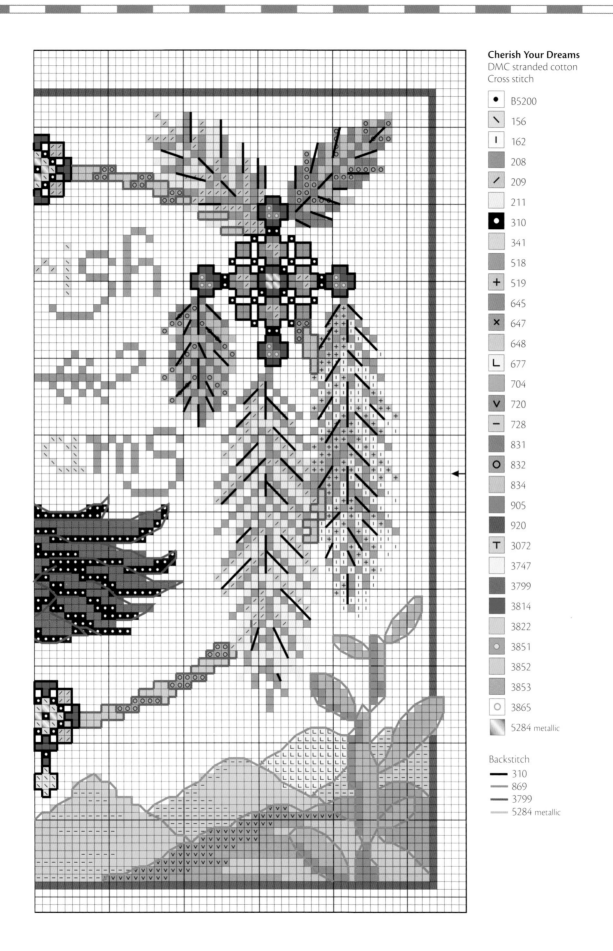

Cherish Your Dreams
DMC stranded cotton
Cross stitch

•	B5200
\	156
I	162
	208
/	209
	211
◉	310
	341
	518
+	519
	645
×	647
	648
L	677
	704
V	720
−	728
	831
O	832
	834
	905
	920
T	3072
	3747
	3799
	3814
	3822
⊙	3851
	3852
	3853
O	3865
⬚	5284 metallic

Backstitch
— 310
— 869
— 3799
— 5284 metallic

DMC stranded cotton
Cross stitch

• blanc	▼ 433	645	V 739	T 783	╲ 3046
L 167	434	╱ 648	✕ 743	844	3047
• 310	I 436	728	746	945	3072
350	437	738	775	3045	

Backstitch

— 310
— 801
— 869

French knots

● 310

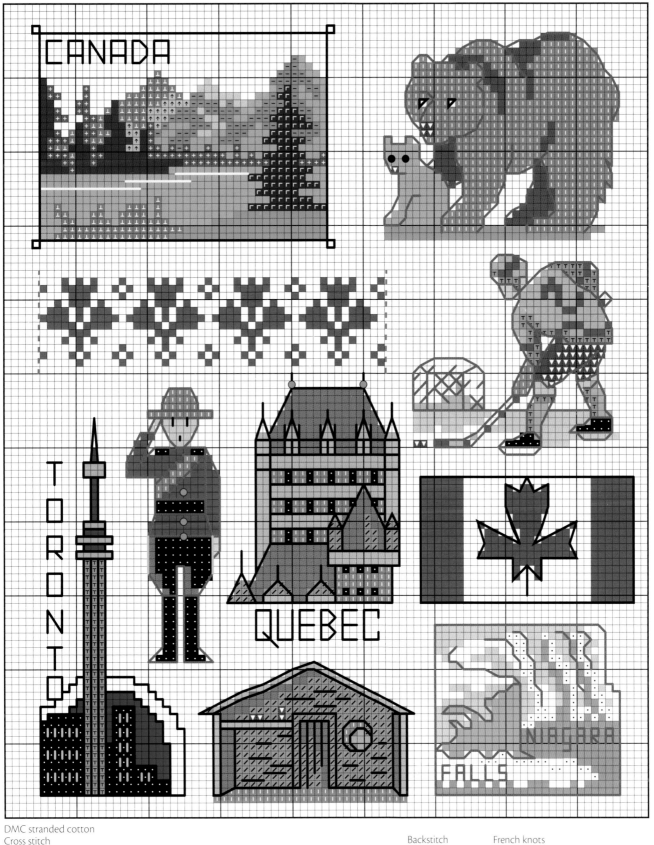

CANADA

TORONTO

QUEBEC

NIAGARA FALLS

DMC stranded cotton
Cross stitch

• blanc	225	▼ 433	505	✏ 648	T 783	⌐ 3818	
⊥ 155	• 310	434	+ 562	704	3072		
– 209	312	I 436	564	728	3747		
210	349	437	645	775	3755		

Backstitch

⎯⎯ blanc

⎯⎯ 310

⎯⎯ 728

⎯⎯ 801

French knots

● 310

● 783

- - - - border pattern repeat

DMC stranded cotton
Cross stitch

- blanc
/ ecru
167
225

· 310
350
I 676
\ 726

797
— 798
3024
3078

3820

Backstitch

blanc
— 310
— 898

French knots

● 310

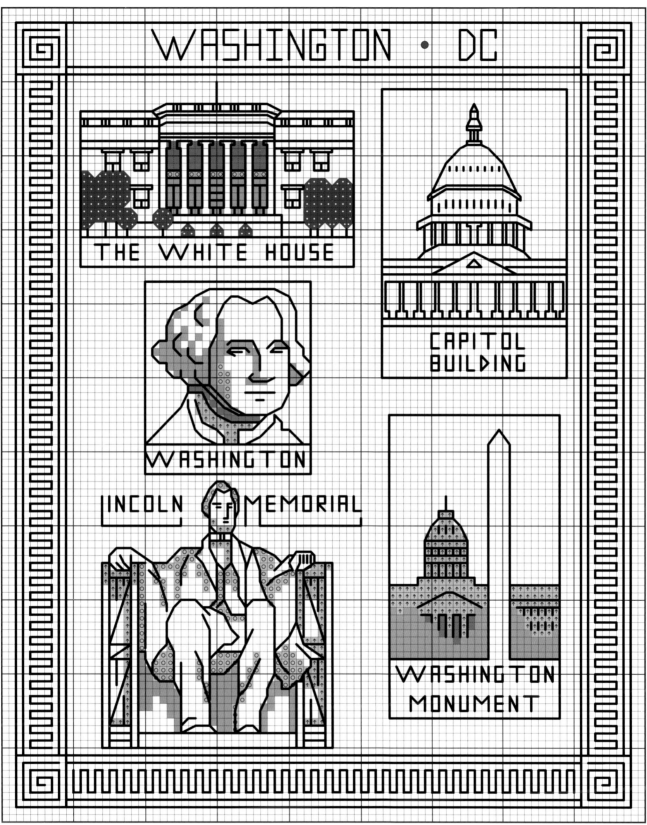

DMC stranded cotton
Cross stitch

○ 168   ▨ 413
  169   ↑ 3072
• 310

Backstitch
——— 310

French knots
● 310

THE MAYFLOWER

NEW ENGLAND

DMC stranded cotton
Cross stitch

- blanc
- 310
- 349
- 433
- 434
- 435
- 517
- 646
- 647
- 648
- 712
- 720
- 726
- 742
- 822
- 844
- 904
- 920
- 945
- 989

Backstitch

— 310
— 801
— 918

- - - border pattern repeat

NEW YORK

EMPIRE STATE

I ♥ NY

CHRYSLER

HAVE A NICE DAY

DMC stranded cotton
Cross stitch

- • blanc
- ▬ 349
- 743
- 3838

- 300
- 436
- 797

- ✚ 301
- ↑ 437
- 905

- • 310
- 648
- ✗ 3024

Backstitch

- ▬ 300
- ▬ 310
- ▬ 349

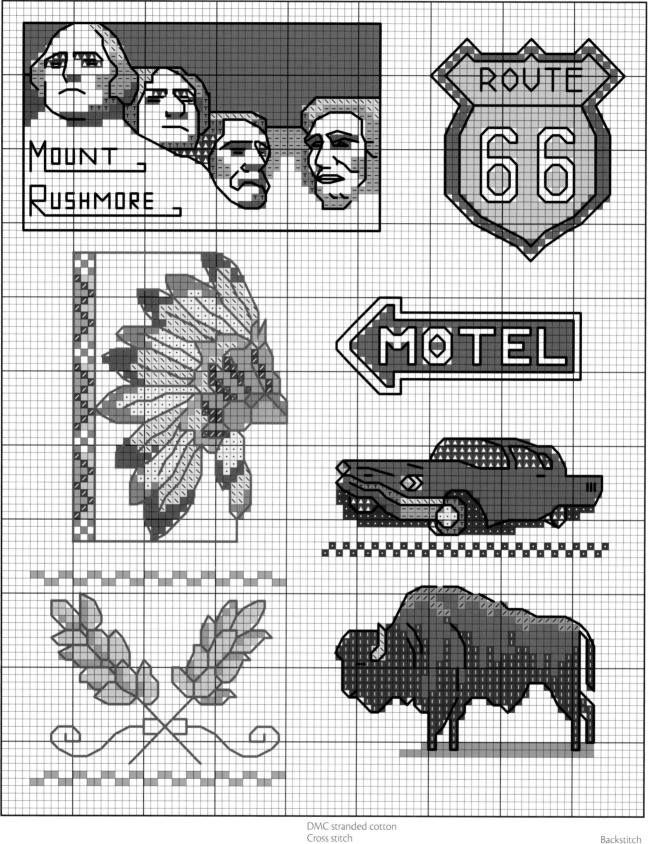

DMC stranded cotton
Cross stitch

Backstitch

• blanc	435	646	826	3852	—— 310	
• 310	/ 437	\ 712	/ 920	3853	—— 433	
350	597	725	T 3023			
I 433	— 644	738	△ 3787			

DMC stranded cotton
Cross stitch

• blanc	◄ 420	703	869	3828
225	519	L 704	3072	⌐ 3852
• 310	647	744	► 3820	
349	700	⊥ 772	3821	

Backstitch

— 310
— 355
— 647
— 898

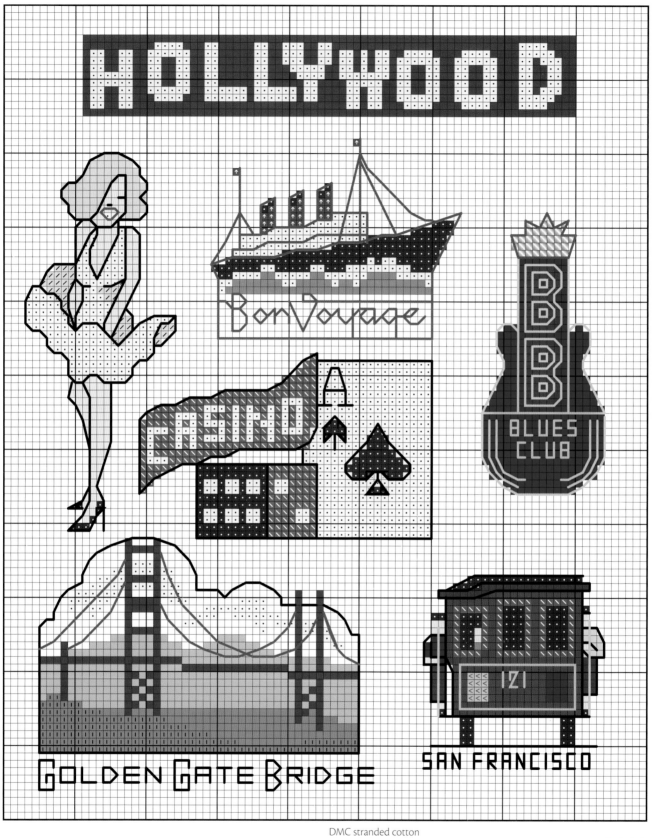

HOLLYWOOD

BonVoyage

CASINO

B B B
BLUES
CLUB

GOLDEN GATE BRIDGE

SAN FRANCISCO

DMC stranded cotton
Cross stitch

					Backstitch
• blanc		704	819	3842	—— 310
• 310	772	905	5282 metallic	—— 725
↑ 347	813	3078		—— 801
\ 350	817	/ 3756		—— 817

DMC stranded cotton
Cross stitch

Backstitch

• blanc	• 310	436	✗ 729	╲ 775	975	⋀ 3826
164	312	→ 676	∟ 739	▼ 782	3022
225	⌐ 334	– 677	743	817	3024
⊥ 300	351	703	760	905	3787

Backstitch

—— 310
—— 729
—— 975
—— 3024

MISSISSIPPI
STEAMER

ST LOUIS ST LOUIS

MISSOURI

DMC stranded cotton
Cross stitch

•	blanc	I	351	✕	800		3072
╱	169		413		834		3828
⊡	310	—	420	▲	869		3852
	349		797		948		5282 metallic

Backstitch

—— 310
—— 349
—— 898
—— 3072

DMC stranded cotton
Cross stitch

• blanc	168	349	727	905	3756
153	169	369	742	951	3804
155	310	703	800	986	3819
167	334	726	892	996	3842

Backstitch

blanc

310

349

898

DMC stranded cotton
Cross stitch

	ecru		422		720		3024
	167		535		728		3812
	310		646		782		3842
	400		677		918		

Backstitch

— ecru
— 310
— 918

French knots or beads
● dark blue

DMC stranded cotton
Cross stitch

• blanc	━ 326	435	˥ 738	3747	⊥ 3834
╱ ecru	335	437	822	3766	3835
❙ 301	349	⊥ 613	905	◥ 3831	3855
◖ 310	▲ 433	704	977	∟ 3833	

Backstitch
— 310
— 326
— 905
— 938

French knots
⬤ 728

SOUTH AMERICA

South America stretches from the tropics to Antarctica, from the damp heat of the Equator to the cold of Cape Horn. Here you will find countries of astonishing colour and contrast: cricket and calypso in the Caribbean; the mighty Amazon basin and its wildlife; the towering mountain ranges of Peru; the elegant Argentinean capital, Buenos Aires, the birthplace of the tango, and the snow fields of Patagonia further south.

What could be a better title for the main picture of this chapter than 'A South American Adventure'? This shows some of the wonderful birds and flowers found in the tropical forests. There's a scarlet macaw, a toucan and a hummingbird, hovering ready to collect the nectar from a hibiscus flower with its long bill. In the background are the Andes, the great mountain chain that towers over the ancient ruined

Inca city of Machu Picchu, built hundreds of years ago.

You will find other traditional Peruvian designs to stitch in this chapter: the Peruvian design on page 54 makes a fun postcard, and the ancient symbols on page 55 are perfect for decorating a notebook or a towel.

Brazil's exuberant Mardi Gras is celebrated in a sampler on page 56: I took one of its motifs to edge a dressing table mat. A Brazilian footballer makes the perfect finishing touch for a boy's kit bag, while the Tango dancers on page 59 are more suitable for a dance bag. If you prefer the laid-back pace of life in the Caribbean, settle down to stitch the delightful hammock postcard from page 53. Let's discover more of this lively and colourful continent…

Peruvian comfort postcard

Make a fun, quick greeting using the chart on page 54. Trim the fabric four squares away from the design, pull out a few threads in a fringe and and attach it with double-sided tape to 6.5 x 9cm (2½ x 3½in) of contrasting yellow card. Work the design on red Aida to avoid having to stitch any background.
Design size 5 x 6.7cm (2 x 2¾in) **Stitch count** 28 x 37

A South American Adventure

Stitch this colourful scene as a reminder of a South American trip. The design is worked on pale blue Aida. Work all the cross stitch before adding any backstitch. Press your completed stitching carefully before framing. A simple wooden frame and blue mount provided the perfect contrast for this design.
Design size 25 x 20cm (9¾ x 8in) **Stitch count** 112 x 140

COLOURFUL
SOUTH AMERICA

Lazy days

Leave all your worries behind when you stitch this idyllic Caribbean beach scene. It makes a perfect fun, quick card. Stitch the design from the chart on page 53 on white Aida and mount it in a bright yellow card with a 7 x 6cm (2¾ x 2¼in) aperture.
Design size 6 x 5cm (2½ x 2in) **Stitch count** 33 x 26

Aztec activity

This Peruvian design makes a striking but simple motif to decorate a plain notebook. Trim to size before fraying the edges and attaching to the book with double sided tape (see page 103)
Design size 5.6 x 6.5cm (2¼ x 2½in)
Stitch count 30 x 36

Perfectly groomed

The blooms on page 52 make an attractive decoration for a clothes brush designed to hold a piece of needlecraft. Work three repeats of the pattern on pale yellow Aida, back your stitching with lightweight iron-on interfacing and trim to fit the exact size of the brush aperture. Assemble following the manufacturer's instructions.
Design size to fit brush 12 x 2.8cm (4¾ x 1⅛in)
Stitch count to fit brush 66 x 15

Bedroom style

The corner motif from the Mardi Gras sampler on page 56 makes an attractive design for a dressing table mat. The design was stitched over two threads on Zweigart Juliana evenweave (ice blue 5506) and will suit the more experienced stitcher as it contains fractional stitches. Start stitching from the corner then trim the fabric to size and fringe the edges by pulling out a few threads all round.

Design size for corner motif 4.7 x 6.6cm (4¼ x 2⅝in)
Stitch count 59 x 36

Ancient symbol

The distinctive Peruvian bird motif on page 55 looks stunning stitched on a towel. The design was worked in the centre of the Aida panel on a cream ready-to-stitch towel.

Design size 3.5 x 6.2cm (1½ x 2½in) **Stitch count** 20 x 34

Football crazy

Decorate a boy's kit bag with the design of a South American player charted on page 57. The design was stitched on emerald green Aida to save stitching the background, trimmed to size, fringed by pulling out a few threads all round, and sewn to the front of a gathered fabric bag. You can stitch the player's strip in colours to match a favourite team.

Design size 6.5 x 5cm (2½ x 2in) **Stitch count** 35 x 27

A South American Adventure
DMC stranded cotton
Cross stitch

Symbol	DMC	Symbol	DMC	Symbol	DMC
•	blanc	◆	310		725
	156	L	341		740
	165	O	349	I	741
	169		413	Y	742
+	744		799	C	907
	745		900		946
	797	↑	905	–	963
▽	798		906		977
	986		3354		3799
▲	3045		3731	←	3803
˥	3046	/	3733		3807
T	3348		3747		3826
×	3827	O	3855		

Backstitch
- 167
- 310
- 413
- 3803
- blanc

BAHAMAS

CUBA

JAMAICA

DMC stranded cotton
Cross stitch

• blanc	L 167	350	I 712	743	986	+ 3756		
153	169	517	⊥ 720	898	3078	3828		
✕ 155	● 310	519	T 728	— 905	⌐ 3608	3853		
╱ 162	I 349	703	▼ 729	╲ 928	3746			

Backstitch
══ blanc
── 898

French knots
● 310

WISH YOU WERE HERE

DMC stranded cotton
Cross stitch

• blanc	350	550	▼ 729	3805
208	⌐ 436	703	− 905	3828
211	445	▲ 704	╲ 917	
I 349	519	T 728	+ 3756	

Backstitch

═══ blanc

─── 898

French knots

◯ 728

- - - - border pattern repeat

PERU

BOLIVIA

MACHU PICCHU

DMC stranded cotton
Cross stitch

				Backstitch
• blanc	■ 433	677	■ 828	◥ 920	—— 310
◦ 310	■ 517	T 703	■ 844	— 3810	—— 433
■ 349	597	✓ 729	■ 904	3828	—— 746
L 420	— 676	I 746	■ 905		

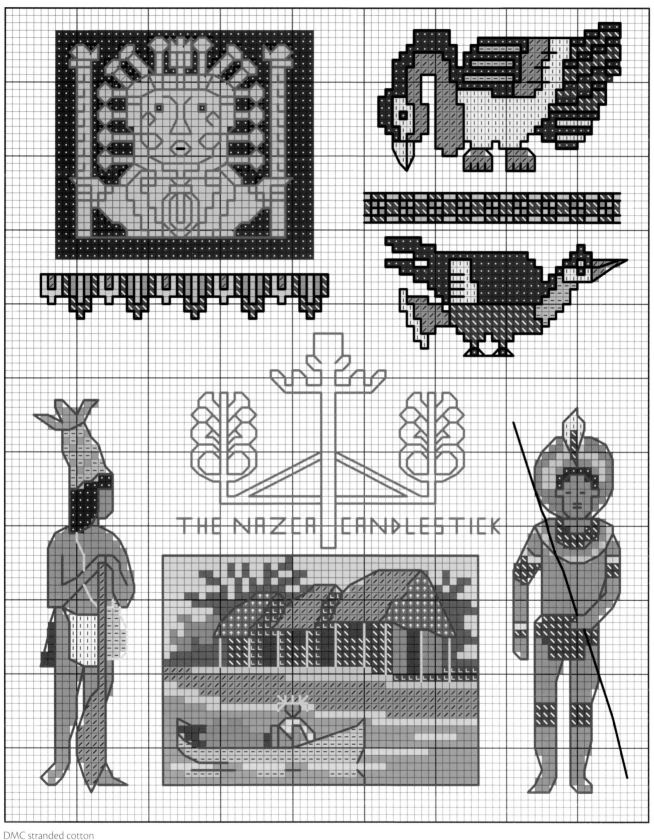

THE NAZCA CANDLESTICK

DMC stranded cotton
Cross stitch

●	310		677	I	746		905
L	420	↑	680		828	╲	920
	597		728		898		922
─	676	╱	729		904		3828

Backstitch

— 310
— 746
— 898
— 920

DMC stranded cotton
Cross stitch

•	blanc		728		807		3746		3837
•	310		738		828		3766		3853
—	437		745		898		3812		
I	517	I	746		3607		3819		

	Madeira Glissen Gloss GR2 80	
	Anchor Reflecta 300	

Backstitch
———	310
———	898
———	Anchor Reflecta 300

French knots
◉	Anchor Reflecta 300

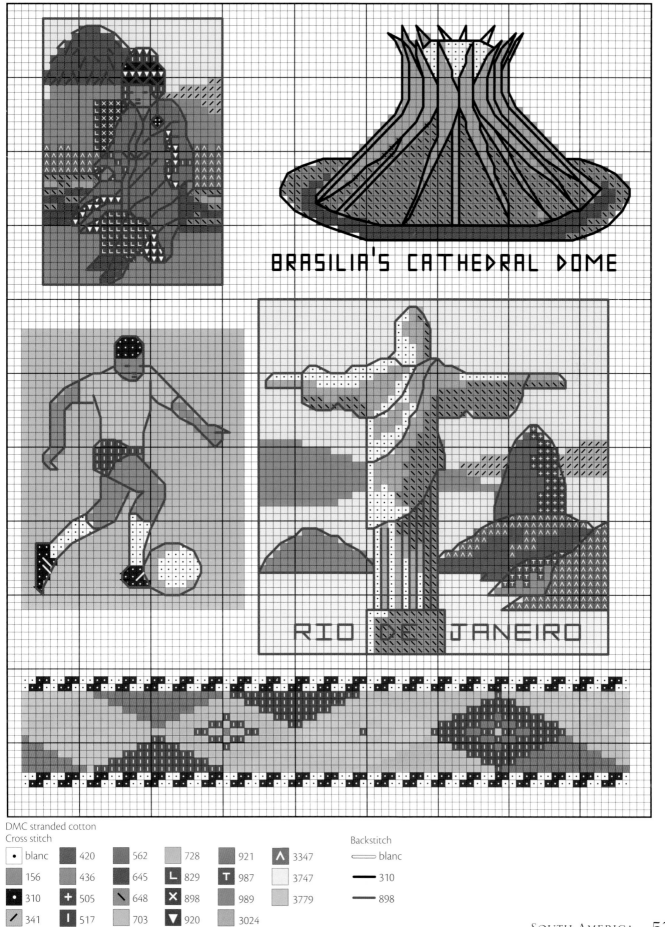

BRASILIA'S CATHEDRAL DOME

RIO DE JANEIRO

DMC stranded cotton
Cross stitch

• blanc	420	562	728	921	∧ 3347
156	436	645	L 829	T 987	3747
⊡ 310	+ 505	648	✕ 898	989	3779
╱ 341	I 517	╲ 648	▼ 920	3024	
		703			

Backstitch

⬯ blanc	
—— 310	
—— 898	

CHILE

DMC stranded cotton
Cross stitch

● 310	645	807	↘ 920	3024	3854	
349	／ 648	819	⊥ 921	3766	↘ 3865	
⊤ 433	728	828	− 987	3838		
435	797	895	988	⊤ 3839		

Backstitch
⊂⊃ blanc
—— 310
—— 898

ARGENTINA

CORDOBA

JUJUY-SAN SALVADOR

DMC stranded cotton
Cross stitch

• blanc	⊥ 433	519	918	— 928	3819	
+ 169	434	744	\ 920	986	3854	
• 310	⊙ 435	898	✕ 922	3607		
350	517	905	927	3774		

Backstitch

— 310
— 744
— 898
— 928

AFRICA

Africa is the second largest continent in the world and home to many diverse peoples, flora and fauna. I have tried to capture the flavour of some of its magnificent sights – from the Egyptian monuments on the banks of the River Nile, to the breathtaking wildlife of the East African Savannah and the unspoilt paradise of the Seychelles – and the people who live there.

I called the main picture for this chapter 'African Beauty'. It's a portrait of an African woman watching yellow-billed storks flying overhead. A safari was one of the first themes that sprang to mind when I was planning my African picture, so I drew giraffes grazing on the Savannah and the distant mountains of East Africa as a backdrop. But the graceful birds add a different perspective to the scene and link the various elements of the design. The natural earthy shades of the woman's clothes and pots match those in the landscape beyond. I did use some artistic licence by adding more colour to the yellow-billed storks.

This chapter also includes two samplers – one celebrating Egyptian civilization and the other a patchwork of bold, contemporary motifs and patterns. You can stitch the whole sampler or take elements to decorate items such a notebook or a wooden bowl. You will also find plenty of motifs featuring African wildlife that will make stunning gifts like the lion desk stand. Finally, for a fun, quick gift, try the tribal bookmark or the frog gift tag. So come with me on an African trip of a lifetime…

Out of Africa

Make a quick greeting by stitching the design on page 71 on Rustico Aida. Using this fabric with the earthy colours in the design gives the flavour of Africa. Trim the fabric five holes away from the design and pull out a few threads all round in a fringe. Stick it to a cream card measuring 7.5 x 9.5cm (3 x 3¾in).
Design size 6.4 x 8.1cm (2½ x 3¼in) **Stitch count** 35 x 45

African Beauty

This large design is stitched on Rustico Aida using beautiful earthy shades of terracotta, brown and blue cotton with some areas highlighted in Krienik 202HL Aztec gold metallic thread. Work all the cross stitch before adding the backstitch. The necklace, earrings and bracelets are represented by seed beads. Add each bead with a half cross stitch in matching thread following the chart.
Design size 24 x 19cm (9¼ x 7½in) **Stitch count** 130 x 104

AFRICAN SAFARI

African style

The border pattern from the Egyptian sampler on page 67 makes a bold decoration for a plain box. Stitch enough of the pattern to span the width of your box lid on Rustico Aida, joining the two ends to make a semi circle and positioning this in the centre as shown. Trim the stitched piece to size allowing enough extra fabric at each end to tuck under the lip of the box lid. Pull out a few threads above and below the design in a fringe and attach the border with double-sided tape.

Design size 3.3 x 15cm (1⅜ x 6in) **Stitch count** 18 x 84

Frog greetings

Make a fun gift tag or quick card using the colourful frog motif from page 73. The design was stitched on white Aida, trimmed three squares away from the edge and fringed by pulling out a few threads. The tag was made from 6.5 x 7.5cm (2½ x 3in) of blue card punched with a hole in the top for the ribbon and the design was attached with double-sided tape.

Design size 4 x 5cm (1½ x 2in) **Stitch count** 21 x 26

Pots of fun

Make a fun gift using the Guinea fowl motif from the sampler on page 69. The design was stitched over two threads on Zweigart Jazlyn linen, (English Rose 4011) and mounted in the lid of a 9cm (3½in) wooden pot following the manufacturer's instructions.

Design size to fit pot lid 4 x 4.2cm (1⅝ x 1⅝in) **Stitch count** 22 x 23

On the wild side

The lion's head from page 70 looks stunning displayed in a wooden desk set, and will make an attractive gift. The design was stitched on cream Aida, trimmed to size and mounted in the round aperture following the manufacturer's instructions. You could also stitch the zebra on page 70 for this gift.

Design size 6 x 5.3cm (2¼ x 2⅛in) **Stitch count** 32 x 29

Tribal colours

Make a tribal carving bookmark using the geometric design on page 71. Stitched on Rustico Aida in strong, earthy colours with no backstitch outlines, this simple design will make an ideal first cross stitch project. Trim your bookmark to size and pull out a few threads on three sides in a fringe and a greater number of threads across the bottom.

Design size 12.5 x 2.5cm (4⅞ x 1in) **Stitch count** 68 x 13

Tutankhamun journal

This stylish motif from page 67 fits beautifully behind the aperture cut into the cover of a notebook you can buy from stationers. The design was stitched on Rustico Aida, trimmed to fit behind the aperture and stuck in place with double-sided tape. You can also stick it to the front of a plain notebook, fringing the edges of your fabric to neaten them. The design is highlighted with Krienik 202HL Aztec gold thread.

Design size 6.4 x 4.4cm (2½ x 1⅝in) **Stitch count** 35 x 24

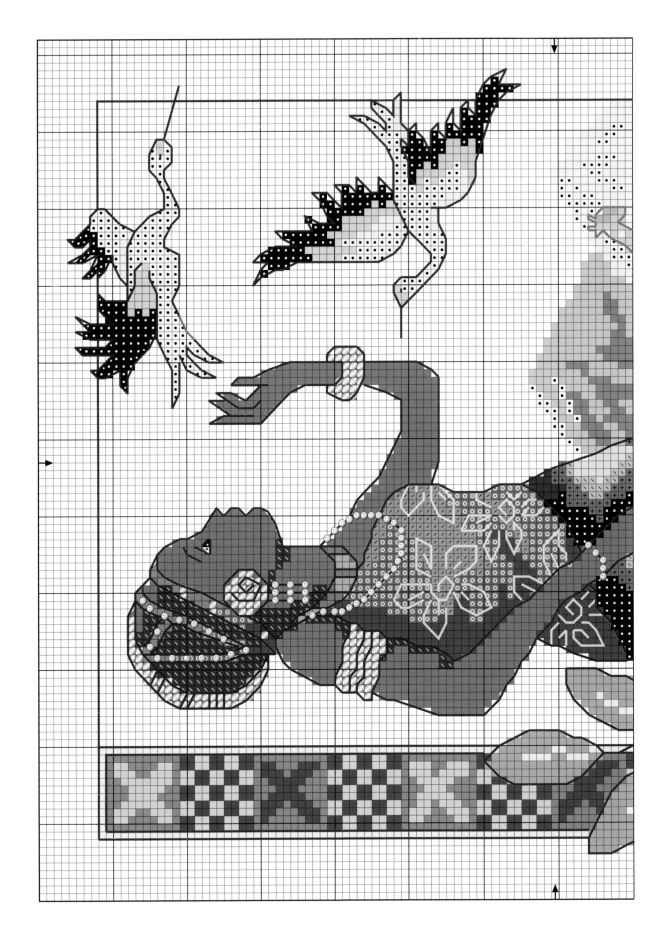

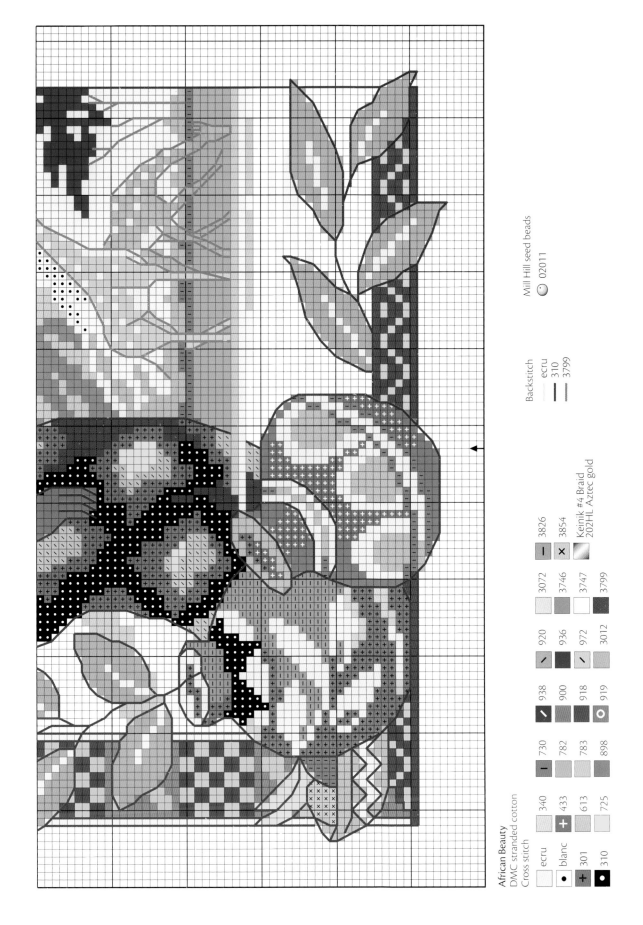

African Beauty
DMC stranded cotton
Cross stitch

ecru	340	433	613	725
blanc ●			
301 +			
310 ●			

938	900	918	919

730	782	783	898

920	936	972	3012

3072	3746	3747	3799

3826	3854

Keinik #4 Braid
202HL Aztec gold

Backstitch
— ecru
— 310
|| 3799

Mill Hill seed beads
◯ 02011

DMC stranded cotton
Cross stitch

■ 158	T 613	– 746	˥ 822	3766	3838
• 310	677	– 782	900	3803	3848
422	728	783	922	3827	＼ 3865
I 550	I 744	L 801	937	／ 3828	

Kreinik 202HL
Aztec gold

Backstitch
— 310
— 898
— Kreinik 202HL Aztec gold

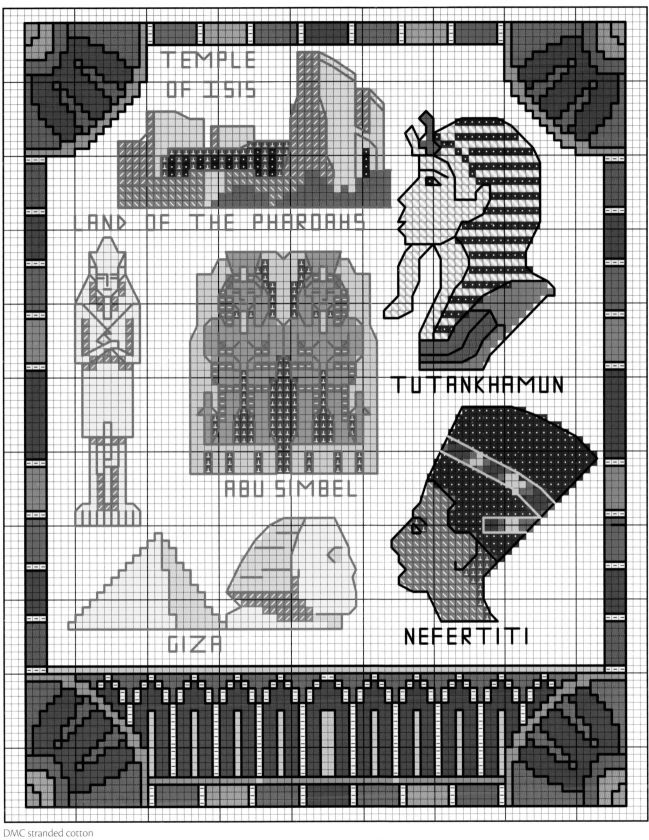

TEMPLE OF ISIS

LAND OF THE PHAROAHS

ABU SIMBEL

GIZA

TUTANKHAMUN

NEFERTITI

DMC stranded cotton
Cross stitch

310	728	783
327	746	900
422	780	922
677	782	937

976	3848
3805	Kreinik 202HL Aztec gold
3828	
3838	

Backstitch

— 310
— 801
— 5282 metallic

DMC stranded cotton
Cross stitch

Backstitch

− 156	350	⊥ 728	780	I 869	3828	— 898
158	• 433	▲ 729	╱ 782	╲ 905	╱ 3865	
208	676	744	783	986	Kreinik 202HL	
341	704	∟ 746	T 807	3766	Aztec gold	

DMC stranded cotton
Cross stitch

				Backstitch
■ 300	■ 680	■ 904	■ 3776	⌐⌐⌐ 746
— 301	■ 704	╲ 905	■ 3814	
╲ 437	■ 738	■ 919	■ 3821	
■ 677	I 745	■ 993	■ 3842	

DMC stranded cotton
Cross stitch

	224		436		646		738		818		3024
	310	Γ	471		648		739	T	822		
	434	I	519	I	712	L	780	/	844		
⊥	435	\	645		734	–	783	⅂	3023		

Half cross stitch

▽ 732
● 734
◆ 869

Backstitch

—— 310
~~~ 356
—— 433
═══ 712

French knots

● 310

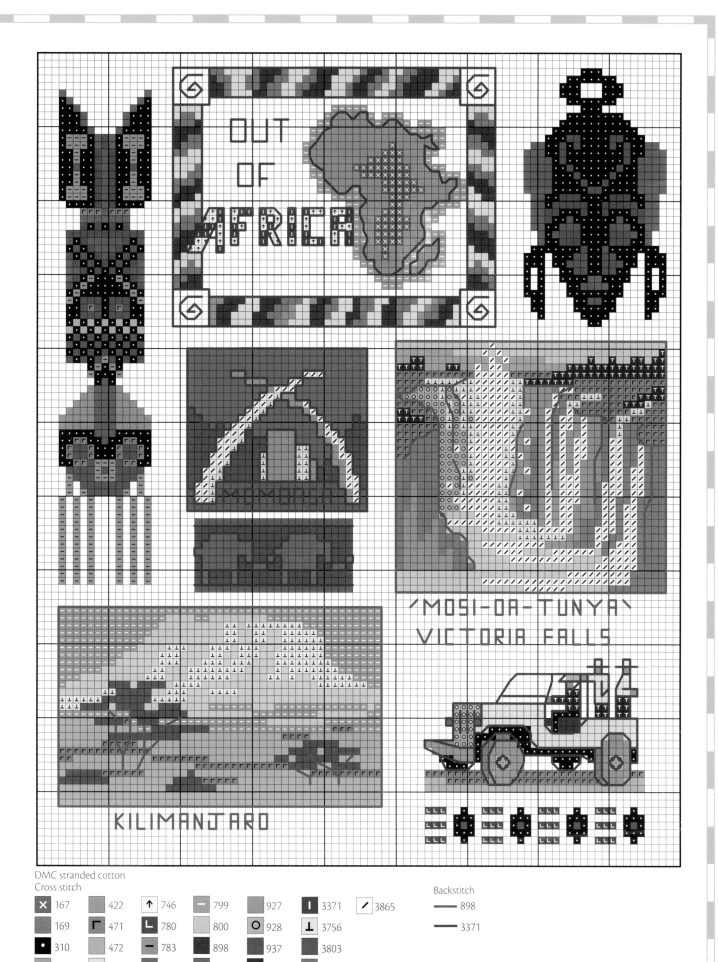

DMC stranded cotton
Cross stitch

✗ 167	422	↑ 746
169	Г 471	L 780
• 310	472	– 783
340	677	798

– 799	927	I 3371
800	O 928	⊥ 3756
898	937	3803
921	T 3345	3828

✗ 3865	

Backstitch

——— 898

——— 3371

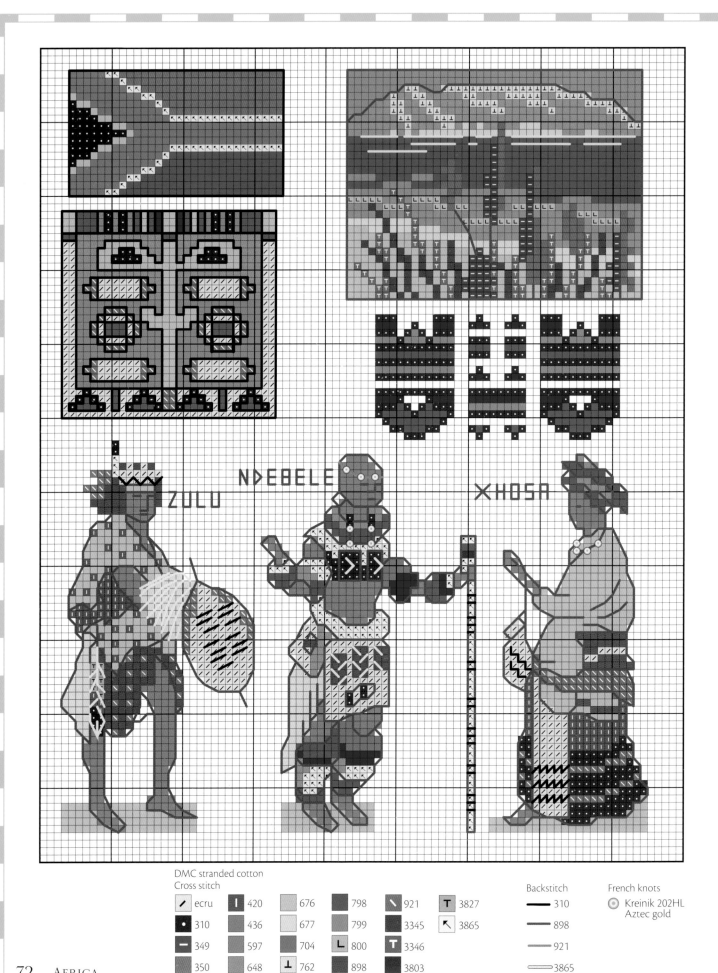

NDEBELE

ZULU

XHOSA

DMC stranded cotton
Cross stitch

/ ecru	I 420	676	798	921	T 3827			
310	436	677	799	3345	3865			
349	597	704	800	T 3346				
350	648	762	898	3803				

Backstitch
—— 310
—— 898
—— 921
═══ 3865

French knots
⊙ Kreinik 202HL
Aztec gold

BAOBAB TREE

DMC stranded cotton
Cross stitch

• blanc	▓ 517	▓ 772	I 827	➤ 922	▓ 3024
● 310	L 646	▓ 780	▓ 905	– 945	N 3755
▓ 350	▓ 704	↑ 782	▓ 907	< 951	➐ 3828
▓ 433	V 746	▓ 819	\ 921	▓ 3023	+ 3852

Backstitch
— 898
— 904
— 3852

French knots
● 310

ASIA

Carpets and camels, temples and pagodas: Asia is a fascinating mix of ancient and modern cultures. This diverse continent stretches from Turkey across the Arabian Desert to the Indian sub continent and on to China and Japan in the east.

My Asian tour takes in such wonders as the magnificent Taj Mahal and the soaring heights of the Himalayas, China's Great Wall and Forbidden City, as well as a Japanese Shinto Temple.

The main design, 'Eastern Promise', is a portrait of a beautiful Japanese woman wearing ceremonial dress. She is surrounded by important symbols of Japanese life and culture: a stunning pagoda, the iconic Mount Fuji and the delicate Wisteria plant, which symbolizes long life, prosperity and good fortune. The chapter also includes several other traditional images of Japan, including a portrait of a Geisha and Japanese martial arts. The fan and orchids on page 88 are perfect for the lid of a wooden box.

I picked India's Taj Mahal, another architectural wonder as the centrepiece for my sampler on page 83. You can take elements of the design to make fun gifts: the ornamental peacocks look good on a gathered bag. Chinese customs also provide plenty of inspiration for designs to stitch. There's a cheeky postcard to send home from a trip, and a cute panda card everyone will love. A fiery red dragon is the ideal embellishment for a red album, and the famous willow pattern makes a nice design for a round coaster. It's time to dip into this wonderful treasure trove of eastern delights…

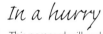

In a hurry

This postcard will make a fun, quick greeting to stitch while you're away. The design was worked on lemon Aida, trimmed six holes away from the design and the edges fringed by pulling out a few threads all round. It was stuck to a 6.5 x 9cm (2½ x 3½in) piece of blue card with double-sided tape.

Design size 4.5 x 7cm (1¾ x 2¾in) **Stitch count** 25 x 39

Eastern Promise

The subtle shade of Parchment 3740 Aida used for the background sets off this Japanese portrait beautifully. The design is finished off with touches of sparkling gold metallic thread (Kreinik #4 gold braid Citron 028). Work all the cross stitch before adding the backstitch outlines and French knots. When all the stitching is complete, press your work carefully and frame, leaving a border of blank fabric around the design.

Design size 25 x 20cm (10 x 8in) **Stitch count** 138 x 112

74

EASTERN DELIGHTS

Turkish bath time

Decorate a towel with the attractive border pattern on page 80. The design is easy to stitch on white Aida band and makes a bold splash of colour against a pale blue towel. Position it in the centre of a length of band to fit the width of your towel, allowing extra for turning under at each end. Machine the band in place on the towel.
Design size as shown 3 x 15.5cm (1⅛ x 6⅛in)
Stitch count 17 x 85

Proud peacocks

These peacocks taken from the Taj Mahal sampler on page 83 are quick to stitch and make a lovely edging for a drawstring bag (see page 104). They were stitched on a cream Zweigart Aida band with a lacy edging and machined to the front of the bag. Cut your band to fit across the bag, allowing extra for turning under each end.
Design size 4.2 x 14.7cm (1¾ x 5⅞in) **Stitch count** 23 x 81

Traditional willow

The simple, traditional blue-and-white willow pattern design from page 86 makes an excellent motif for a coaster. The design was stitched on white Aida and backed with iron-on interfacing to prevent fraying before being trimmed to fit the coaster. Assemble following the manufacturer's instructions .
Design size 5 x 7.7cm (2 x 3in) **Stitch count** 27 x 42

Dragon tales

Use the fiery red Chinese dragon on page 86 to turn an ordinary notebook into something special. The design was worked on a Zweigart natural linen band in stranded cotton and Kreinik #4 gold braid (Citron 028). If you stitch the design on a strip of band twice the length of the notebook plus turnings, you can join the ends with a seam on the back of the cover.

Design size 6.2 x 15cm (2½ x 6in)
Stitch count 34 x 83

Motherly love

Who can resist this card showing an adorable portrait of a mother panda and her baby? The design is charted on page 87 and was stitched on white Aida and mounted in a purple card with a 7.5 x 7cm (3 x 2¾in) aperture.

Design size 6.7 x 6.3cm (2¾ x 2½in) **Stitch count** 37 x 36

Sewing notion

Here's an impressive gift to make for a fellow stitcher. The Oriental fan and orchids motif from page 88 was stitched on antique white Aida and mounted in a wooden scissor box with an oval aperture in the lid. Back your design with iron-on vilene to prevent the fabric edges fraying before trimming it to fit behind the aperture in the box. Assemble following the manufacturer's instructions.

Design size 5.7 x 3.6cm (1½ x 2⅛in) **Stitch count** 20 x 31

Eastern Promise
DMC stranded cotton
Cross stitch

153	469	746	3747	3820
156	676	792	3799	3823
310	677	832	3807	3835
327	729	918	3814	3853
		920		3855
		921		
		945		
		948		

Kreinik #4 Braid
028 citron

Backstitch
— 310
— 350
— 832 (long stitch)
— 3823

French knots
● 310
○ 3823

DMC stranded cotton
Cross stitch

✓ ecru	▨ 349	▨ 703	▨ 822	▬ 3746	
▨ 157	▨ 402	▨ 728	❚ 919	▨ 3812	
▨ 301	◸ 433	◸ 745	▨ 945	L 3855	
⬛ 310	▨ 645	▨ 792	◸ 976	❚ 3865	

Backstitch
— 310
— 433
⟳ 3865

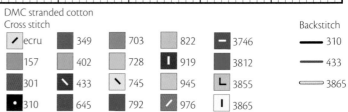

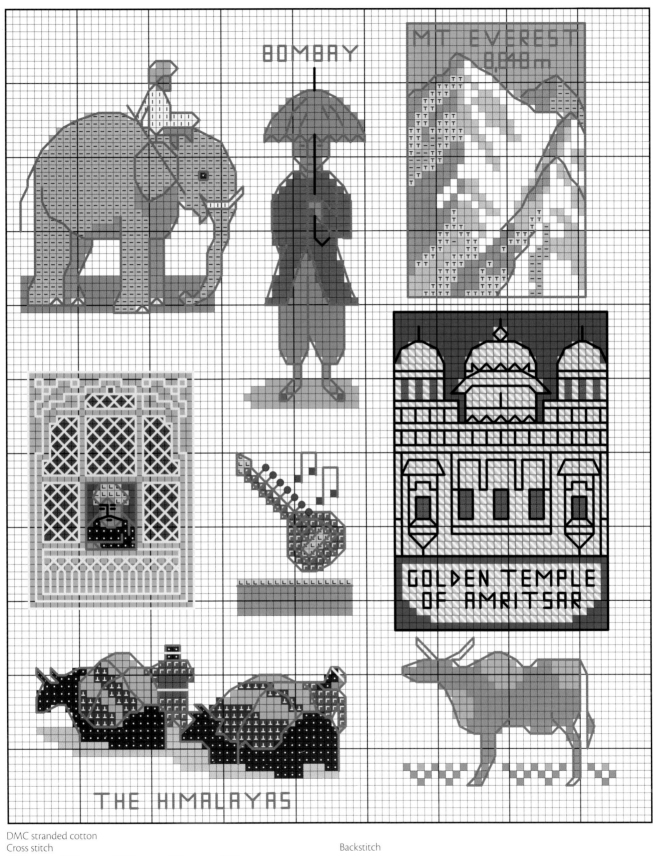

DMC stranded cotton
Cross stitch

— 168	349	703	938	L 3855		
169	422	798	977	I 3865		
310	535	828	T 3756	Kreinik 028 citron		
347	553	Г 921	3766			

Backstitch

— 310

— 938

— 3865

French knots

● 938

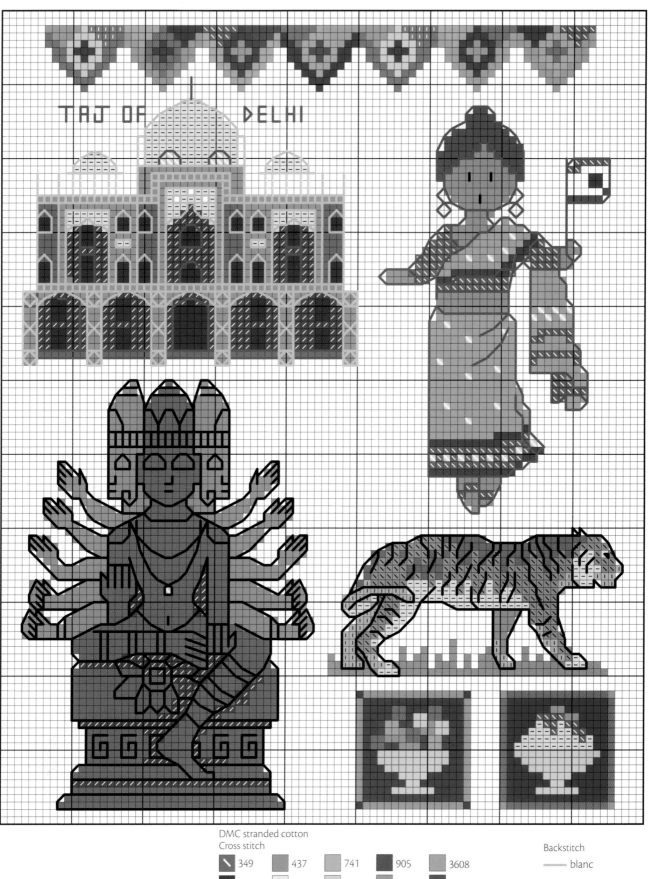

TAJ OF DELHI

DMC stranded cotton
Cross stitch

╲ 349	437	741	905	3608
433	− 712	743	907	3799
╱ 434	734	╲ 783	917	I 3804
435	I 738	798	946	╲ Kreinik 028 citron

Backstitch

— blanc
— 310
— 801
— Kreinik 028 citron

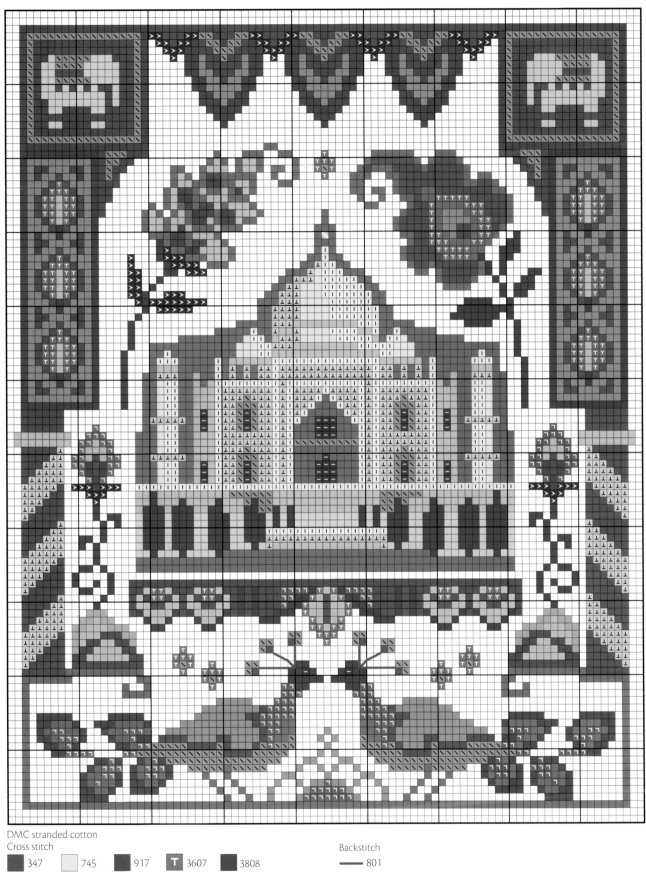

DMC stranded cotton
Cross stitch

Backstitch

347	745	917	3607	3808
552	746	922	3608	3814
728	782	937	3746	3847
744	783	975	3756	Kreinik 028 citron

——— 801

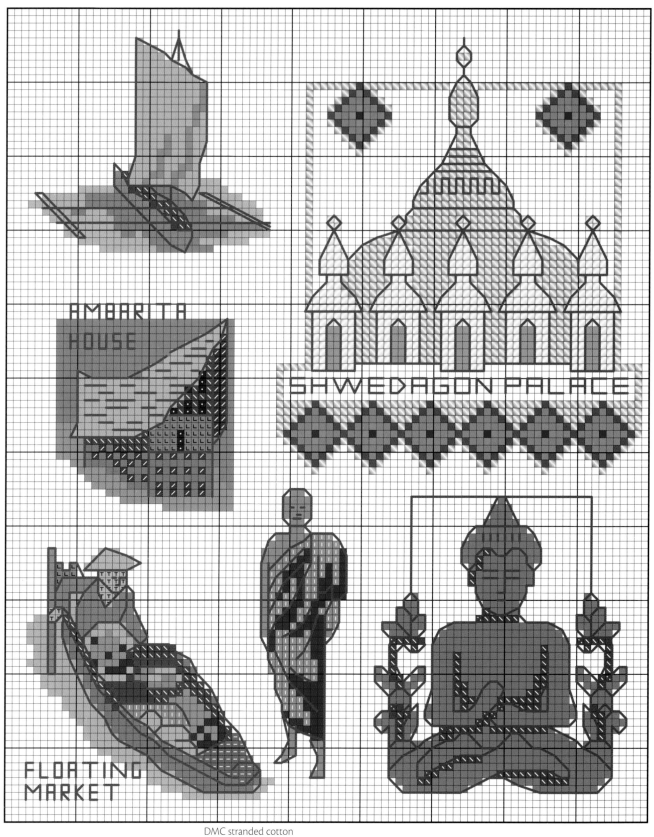

AMBARITA
HOUSE

SHWEDAGON PALACE

FLOATING
MARKET

DMC stranded cotton
Cross stitch

- ● 310
- 322
- 368
- L 422
- ◥ 434
- 435
- 505
- 648
- 729
- ◢ 801
- 920
- I 922
- T 945
- 3047
- 3325
- — 3828

Kreinik 002HL gold

Kreinik 017HL white gold

Backstitch
—— 801

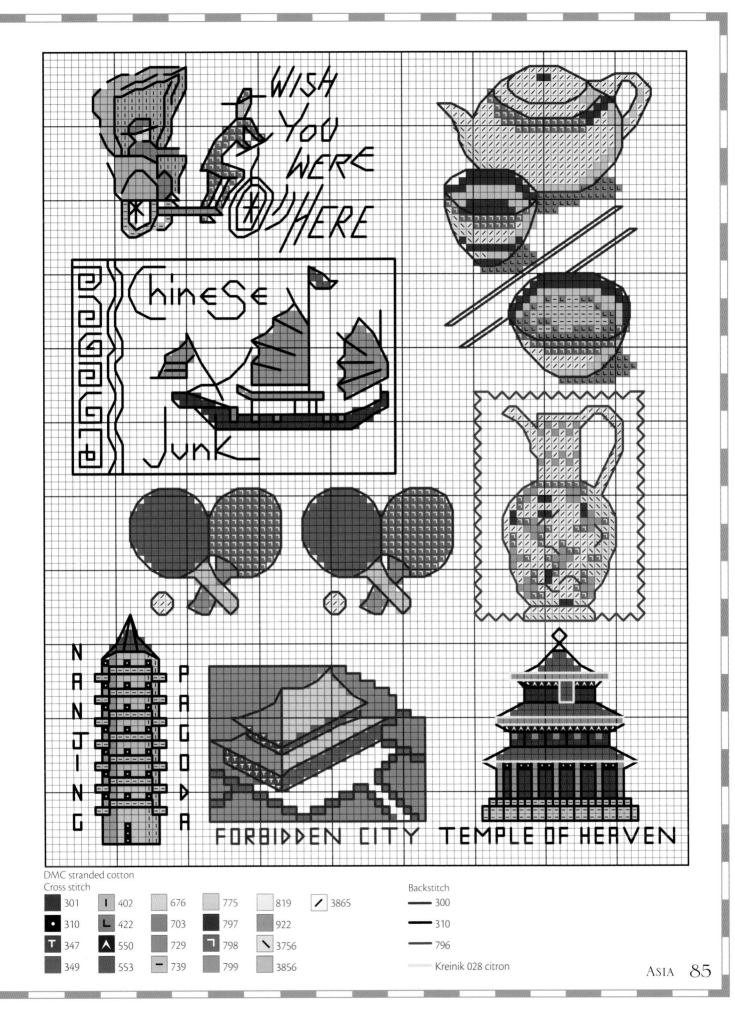

WISH YOU WERE HERE

Chinese Junk

NANJING PAGODA

FORBIDDEN CITY   TEMPLE OF HEAVEN

DMC stranded cotton
Cross stitch

301	I 402	676
• 310	L 422	703
T 347	∧ 550	729
349	553	− 739

775	819	∕ 3865
797	922	
⌐ 798	799	∖ 3756
799	3856	

Backstitch
—— 300
—— 310
—— 796
~~~~ Kreinik 028 citron

DMC stranded cotton
Cross stitch

I	B5200	Ⅴ	356		754		791		832		937
＼	304	＼	471		772	／	798		834	L	3747
	321		677		775		799	ㄱ	920	－	3807
	341	－	746	I	777	T	800	⊥	922		3825

Backstitch
—— 300
—— 310
—— 797
—— Kreinik 028 citron

French knots
● 310

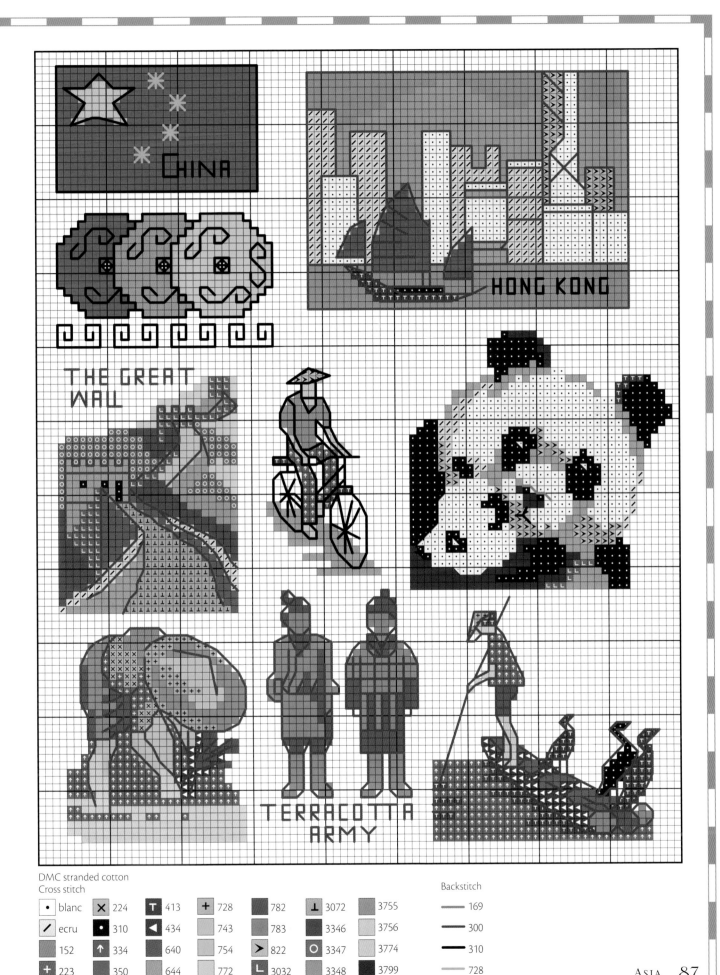

CHINA

HONG KONG

THE GREAT
WALL

TERRACOTTA
ARMY

DMC stranded cotton
Cross stitch

• blanc	✕ 224	T 413	+ 728	782	⊥ 3072	3755
╱ ecru	• 310	◀ 434	743	783	3346	3756
152	↑ 334	640	754	> 822	O 3347	3774
+ 223	350	644	772	L 3032	3348	3799

Backstitch

— 169
— 300
— 310
— 728

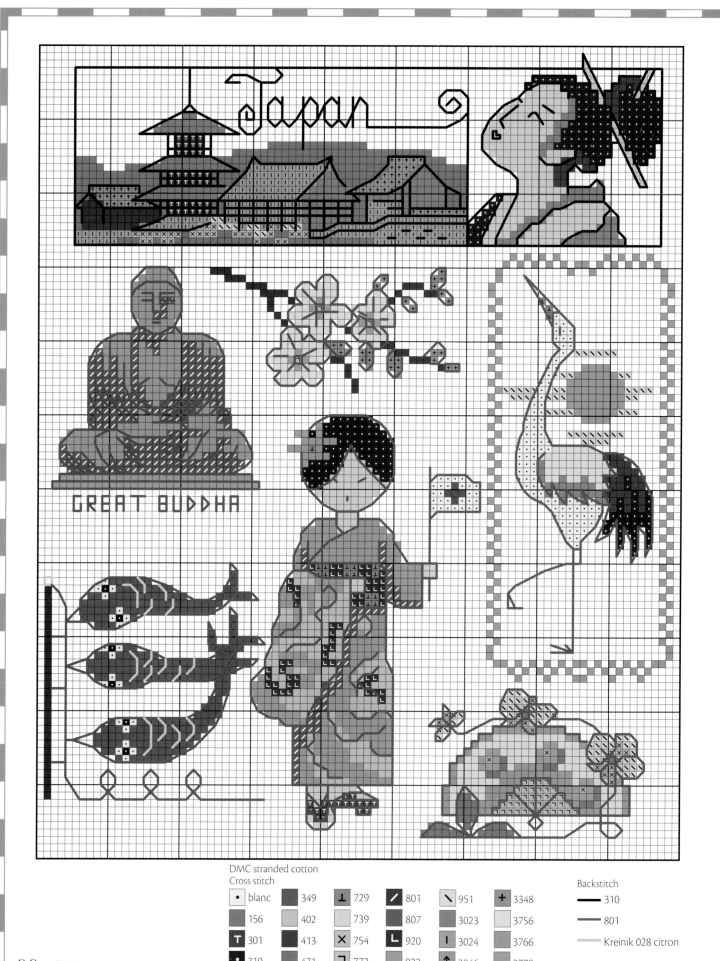

DMC stranded cotton
Cross stitch

• blanc	349	⊥ 729	╱ 801	╲ 951	+ 3348
156	402	739	807	3023	3756
T 301	413	✕ 754	L 920	I 3024	3766
• 310	471	⌐ 772	922	↑ 3046	3778

Backstitch

— 310

— 801

Kreinik 028 citron

HORYUJI   OSAKA   CASTLE

GOLDEN PAVILLION

SUMA
WRESTLER

JUDO

KARATE

TORI
GATE

KUMAMOTO
CASTLE

SHINTO TEMPLE

DMC stranded cotton
Cross stitch

• blanc	422	922	3345	3755	L 3852	
310	676	926	— 3346	3774	Kreinik 028 citron	
— 340	801	✓ 927	+ 3348	3821		
I 420	I 869	3072	3746	＼ 3828		

Backstitch
—— 310
—— 801

AUSTRALASIA

Australasia spans a vast area of the Pacific Ocean, dominated by Australia, New Zealand, Papua New Guinea and many other islands. I have tried to show both the traditional way of life on this continent and modern landmarks like the Sydney Opera House.

Many well-known Australian images are found in the main design, which I called 'The Wonders of Australia'.

There's the cuddly koala and endearing kangaroo, animals unique to Australia, plus the noisy kookaburra bird. Two Australian natural wonders – Uluru, formerly known as Ayers Rock, and the Great Barrier Reef – are also included and the duck-billed platypus, an animal so shy that very few people have actually seen one. These images are drawn against the distinctive shape of a map of Australia and would make a wonderful memento of a trip down under.

Aboriginal paintings provided the inspiration for the sampler on page 97. You can take individual motifs to make small gifts like a luggage label. I used a palette of blue and green for my New Zealand designs on page 98 to represent the temperate climate of this country. The kiwi fruit motif makes a fun fridge magnet, or perhaps you prefer the flightless kiwi bird. The distinctive Maori patterns, strong swirling shapes worked in shades of terracotta, black and cream, make a stunning decoration for table linen. Finally, the Antarctic wilderness and its penguins provide the inspiration for a simple name plaque, and is the perfect place to end our world tour.

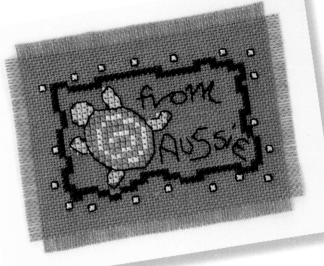

Down under

The turtle greeting on page 97 makes a fun postcard for friends back home. The design was stitched over two threads on natural linen, trimmed 1cm away from the design and fringed by pulling out a few threads, then stuck to a 7.5 x 10cm (3 x 4in) piece of cream card with double-sided tape.

Design size 4.5 x 7.5cm (1¾ x 2⅞in) **Stitch count** 25 x 37

The Wonders of Australia

The blue coastline and the bright colours of Uluru and other images on this design look good against a pale lemon Aida fabric background. Stitch all the cross stitch before adding the backstitch outlines and check you have counted the squares correctly between the motifs. A simple wooden frame and blue mount complement the design beautifully.

Design size 25 x 18.5cm (9⅞ x 7⅞in) **Stitch count** 97 x 134

AROUND
AUSTRALASIA

Kangaroos ahead

This fellow will make a colourful reminder of a trip to Australia every time you take a sip of tea if you pop him in a coaster. The design is charted on page 96 and was stitched on yellow Zweigart Cashel linen, backed with iron-on interfacing to prevent fraying and trimmed to fit the coaster. Assemble following the manufacturer's instructions.

Design size 8.1 x 8.1cm (3¼ x 3¼in) **Stitch count** 45 x 45

Jumping jellyfish

You can take the motifs from the sampler on page 97 to make a number of small gifts. The simple jellyfish in the top right corner is perfect for a keyring. The design was stitched on parchment Aida, backed with interfacing and trimmed to fit the aperture. Assemble following the manufacturer's instructions.

Design size 3.8 x 4cm (1½ x 1½in) **Stitch count** 21 x 22

Sweet scented lily

The Mount Cook lily motif from page 99 looks pretty stitched on an Aida band in a contrasting shade of red and made into a sachet. The stitched piece was folded in half and sewn up into a sachet, as explained on page 104.

Design size 7.5 x 4cm (3 x 1½in) **Stitch count** 43 x 22

Table elegance

The bold Maori pattern from page 99 makes a stunning decoration for a placemat. It was stitched on Zweigart Jazlyn linen in willow green 3014. Cut your fabric to size and stitch the design out from the centre to each side. Back your stitching with iron-on interfacing cut slightly smaller than the mat, and fringe the edges up to the start of the interfacing.

Design size 2 x 16cm (¾ x 6⅜in)
Stitch count 12 x 91

Juicy kiwi

The kiwi fruit charted on page 98 makes a fun fridge magnet for the kitchen. The design was stitched on white Aida, backed with iron-on interfacing to prevent fraying and trimmed to fit the fridge magnet. Assemble following the manufacturer's instructions, checking the design is correctly positioned before snapping shut.

Design size 2.5 x 2.2cm (1 x ⅞in) **Stitch count** 14 x 12

Penguin parade

The Antarctic penguins on page 101 make an ideal decoration for a child's room plaque. The design was stitched on sky blue Aida. Map out your penguins on graph paper first leaving a few blank squares between each one. Use the alphabet on page 102 to spell out the name underneath. Press your work carefully and frame as a picture.

Design size for picture shown
9 x 13cm (3½ x 5⅛in)
Stitch count for picture shown 48 x 67

NORTH

ULURU

WESTERN

SOUTH

Ne

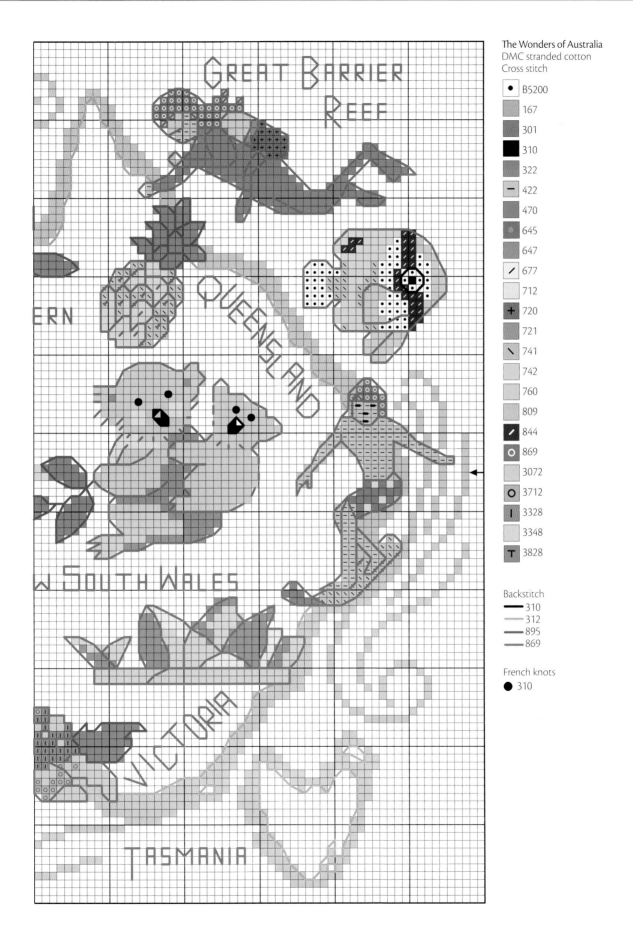

The Wonders of Australia
DMC stranded cotton
Cross stitch

- • B5200
- 167
- 301
- 310
- 322
- − 422
- 470
- 645
- 647
- ╱ 677
- 712
- ✛ 720
- 721
- ╲ 741
- 742
- 760
- 809
- ╱ 844
- ⊙ 869
- 3072
- ⊙ 3712
- I 3328
- 3348
- T 3828

Backstitch
——— 310
‒‒‒ 312
——— 895
——— 869

French knots
● 310

DMC stranded cotton
Cross stitch

• blanc	• 310	728	824	986		
⊥ 162	321	I 782	/ 825	L 987		
168	• 413	T 783	826	988		
\ 169	472	– 813	975			

Backstitch
⊂⊃ blanc
— 310

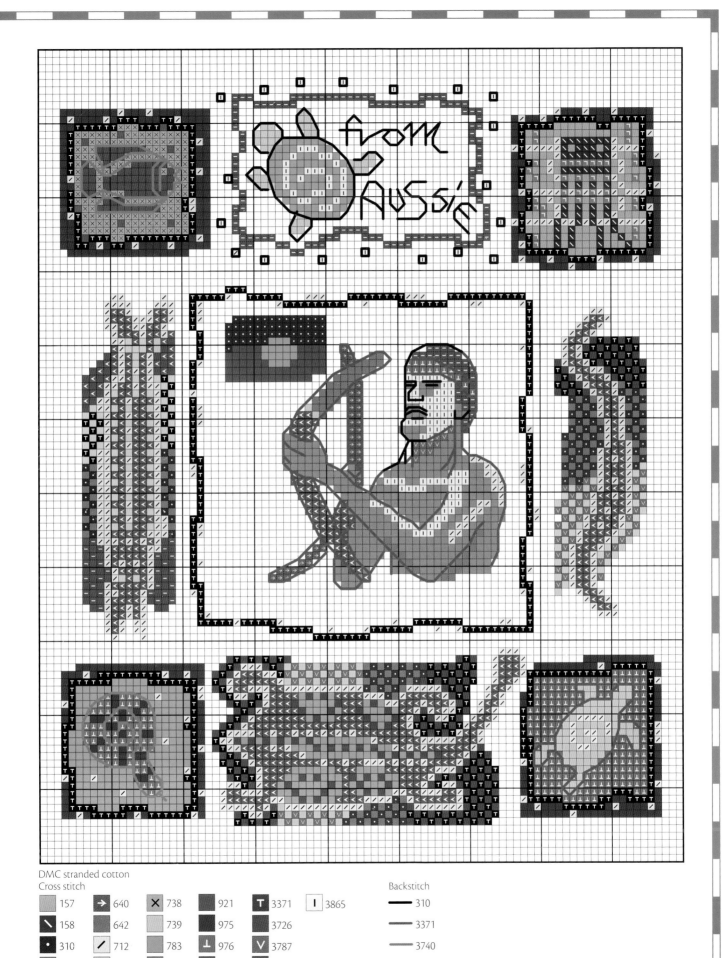

DMC stranded cotton
Cross stitch

	157	→	640	✕	738		921	⊤	3371	I	3865
╲	158		642		739		975		3726		
•	310	╱	712		783	⊥	976		3787		
	422		728	˥	793	◄	3021	─	3799		

Backstitch

─── 310
─── 3371
─── 3740

NEW ZEALAND

WELLINGTON

MOUNT RUAPEHU CHRISTCHURCH

DMC stranded cotton
Cross stitch

• blanc	– 168	413	/ 826	> 898	⌐ 987	
156	169	⊥ 420	L 827	– 921	988	
162	● 310	738	832	975	3047	
＼ 164	+ 341	824	Ɩ 869	986	3821	

Backstitch

— 310
— 472
— 738
— 898

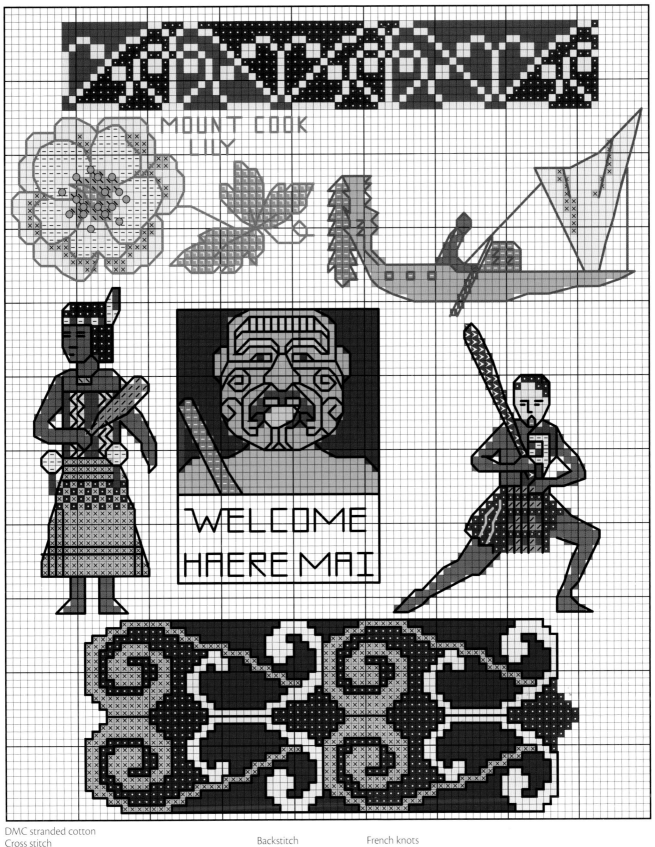

MOUNT COOK
LILY

WELCOME
HAERE MAI

DMC stranded cotton
Cross stitch

╲	164	╱	422	＞	898	⌐	988
•	310		738		920	✕	3047
	402		746	─	921		3777
	420	❘	869		922	－	3865

Backstitch
— 310
— 420
— 898
— 3047

French knots
● 783

PAPUA NEW GUINEA

EASTER ISLAND

TAHITI

DMC stranded cotton
Cross stitch

				Backstitch
• blanc	613	∧ 782	I 869	⌐ 3021	3848	—— 310
164	640	∕ 783	920	⊥ 3817	—— 898
⊙ 310	∕ 642	826	987	L 3821
420	728	– 827	∖ 988	T 3828

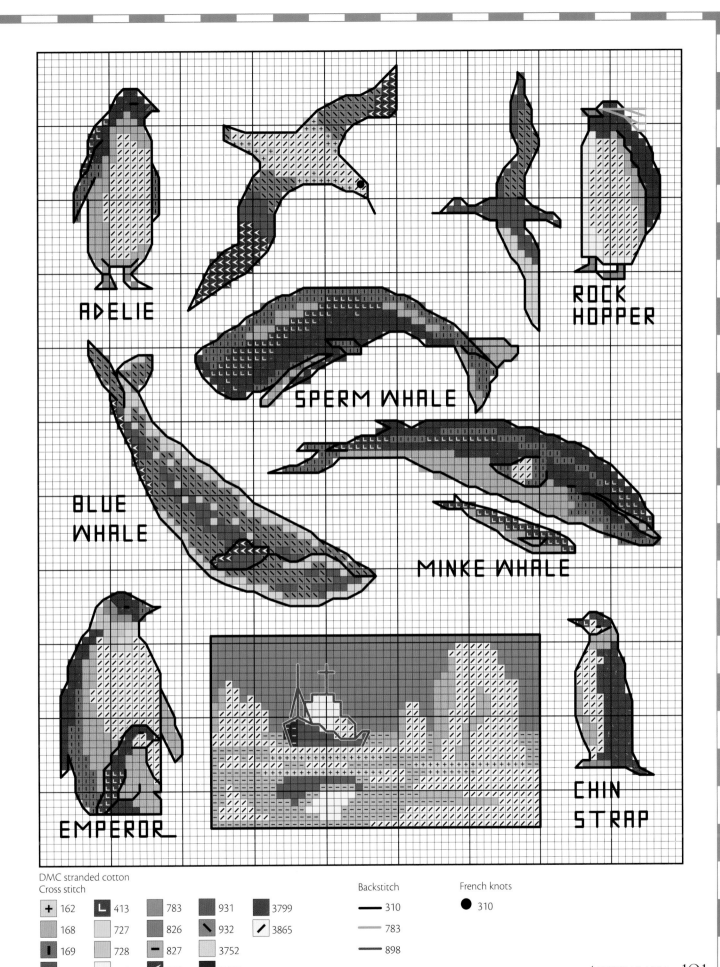

ADELIE

ROCK HOPPER

SPERM WHALE

BLUE WHALE

MINKE WHALE

EMPEROR

CHIN STRAP

DMC stranded cotton
Cross stitch

+ 162	L 413	783	931	3799
168	727	826	✕ 932	✔ 3865
▌ 169	728	▬ 827	930	3752
350	746	◄ 930	▬ 3777	

Backstitch

—— 310

—— 783

—— 898

French knots

● 310

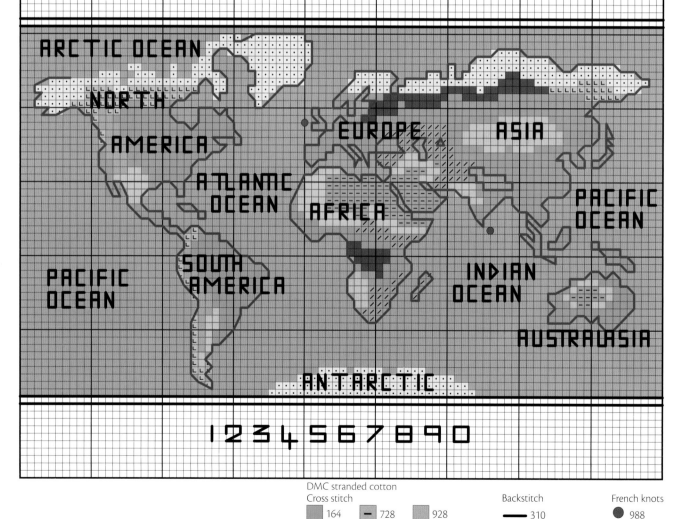

ARCTIC OCEAN

NORTH

AMERICA

EUROPE

ASIA

ATLANTIC
OCEAN

AFRICA

PACIFIC
OCEAN

PACIFIC
OCEAN

SOUTH
AMERICA

INDIAN
OCEAN

AUSTRALASIA

ANTARCTIC

1234567890

DMC stranded cotton
Cross stitch

	164	-	728		928
L	369		743		988
/	472		826	•	3865

Backstitch

—— 310

—— 825

French knots

● 988

MAKING UP THE PROJECTS

Many of the gifts in this book have been mounted in products such as trinket pots, fridge magnets, keyrings and coasters, which you can buy from needlecraft stockists. Follow the manufacturer's instructions to make up these items. In this chapter you will find instructions on how to make up the other projects in the book including the postcards, drawstring bag, sachet and bell pull. You should find the steps quick and easy to follow.

Postcards and tags

Use this technique to make the postcards in each chapter or a simple stitched tag attached with ribbon (see pages 28 and 62).

You will need
- Stitched motif
- Coloured card cut to size
- Double-sided tape

1 Trim your stitched fabric to fit your tag and fringe the edges by pulling out a few threads. If using an Aida band trim the length only.

2 Stick the fabric to the card with double-sided tape and punch a hole in one corner for a ribbon if required.

3 You can stitch the design on plastic canvas instead to decorate a hat (see page 28), or attach your tag to the cover of an album or notebook (see pages 9 and 48).

Greetings cards

Many of the motifs in the book will make ideal cards. Either buy a card mount with an aperture to fit your design or cut your own from a sheet of artist's card.

You will need
- Stitched design
- Card mount to fit
- Double-sided tape or craft glue

1 Trim the edges of your stitching to fit inside the card aperture, leaving enough extra fabric for sticking in place.

2 Make sure the card is the right way up then apply a thin coat of craft glue or double-sided tape around the aperture on the back.

3 Lay the stitching face up on a flat surface and put the card on top. Check the stitching is correctly positioned before pressing down firmly.

4 Fold the spare card flap over the back of the stitching and stick in place with glue or tape.

Album cover

Work the motif on a strip of fabric and sew it around a book cover (see page 77). Use Aida or an Aida band for this.

You will need
- Stitched motif
- Album or notebook

1 Measure the depth of your book and double this figure. Add 2.5cm (1in) extra for joining the strip and cut your fabric this length.

2 Stitch the design in the centre of your band. If using Aida, trim it to size and fringe the top and bottom edges only (see postcards and tags above). Iron lightweight interfacing to the back to stiffen the fabric and keep the stitches in place.

3 Put the strip on the book and fold the ends around the cover. Slipstitch in place, turning the raw edges under.

Bell pull

Bell pulls like the New England church design on page 29 can be made from an Aida band or a strip of Aida.

You will need
- Stitched design
- Bell pull ends

Hem the sides of your fabric if using Aida. Fold over a 5cm (2in) turning at the top and bottom, making sure the raw edges are tucked under. Slipstitch in place, leaving an opening either side of the turning to push the bell pull shaft through. Slip on each end.

Drawstring bags

A drawstring bag is perfect for displaying a motif you have stitched. Either sew your stitched design to a print fabric or cut it to the size required.

You will need
- Stitched design
- Fabric for the bag and matching cord or ribbon

1 Cut two pieces of fabric the right size plus 2.5cm (1in) for seams. Machine or slipstitch your stitching in place on the front if using a print fabric.

2 Put the pieces right sides together and stitch around three sides, 1.5cm (½in) in. Leave the top open and a 5cm (2in) opening on each side at the top.

3 Trim across the bottom corners. Press the side seams open. Turn the top edges over 1.5cm (½in) then 4cm (1½in). Add two lines of machining to form the casing. Thread cord or ribbon through the casing.

Phone pouch

See page 8 for this handy gift.

You will need
- Stitched design
- Popper for fastening

1 Measure the length of your phone and cut your band twice this size, adding 2.5cm (1in) for turnings. Turn under the ends by 1.25cm (½in) and hem.

2 Position the top of the design 4cm (1½in) in from the left edge of the band, and stitch the bee motif two squares in from the right edge.

3 Back your stitching with interfacing and sew up the side seams with neat slipstitches, leaving a 4cm (1½in) flap that folds down. Sew on a popper.

Aida band

Use an Aida band to personalize a towel (see page 76) or spherical object (see page 9).

You will need
- Stitched design
- Towel or pencil holder

1 Measure the towel width or pot circumference and add 2.5cm (1in) extra to cut your band. Fold in half and mark the centre with contrasting tacking.

2 Work out how many repeats of the pattern will fit on your band. Start in the centre and work out to each end.

3 Iron interfacing to the back of the band to stiffen it. Turn under each end and machine or slipstitch to the towel. Slipstitch the ends together around the pot.

sachet or pincushion

You can make a sachet from Aida or Aida band like the ones on pages 9 and 92.

1 Cut two squares of fabric allowing 2cm (¾in) for seams. With right sides facing, pin the front and back together, or fold the Aida band in half.

2 Sew round the edges leaving a gap on one side. Clip the corners and turn through.

3 Fill with wadding or a pot-pourri mixture before sewing up the seam on the right side.

INDEX